The Wild Flowers of Loophead
County Clare, Ireland

Carmel T. Madigan

First published in 2012 by:
Carmel T. Madigan
Creative Studio,
Ballyalla, Ennis,
Co. Clare
IRELAND

www.carmelmadigangallery.com

Text and Poetry © Carmel T. Madigan
Photography © Carmel T. Madigan except 'Eyebright' image p. 43 © & courtesy of Sharon Parr
Digital graphics including maps and botanical illustrations © Carmel T. Madigan
Artwork © Carmel T. Madigan

All rights reserved. No part of this publication may be reproduced, stored
or transmitted in any form without the express permission of the publisher.

The author accepts no responsibility for suggested herbal remedies contained within this book,
which are meant for informational purposes only and not intended to diagnose, treat, cure or prevent any disease.

ISBN: 978 0 9572127 0 1

A copy of this book has been lodged for cataloguing with the British Library.

Design & Layout - Carmel T. Madigan
Printed and bound by Hudson Killeen Ltd, Ballycoolin Business Park, Blanchardstown, Dublin 15.

This publication has been part-funded by the LEADER programme, through the National Development Plan and by the European Agricultural Fund for Rural Development.

Front Cover Artwork: 'Floral Society by the Marshy Way' © Carmel. T. Madigan 2012

CONTENTS

Forewords		5
1	Introduction	11
2	Getting Started	16
3	Open Peaty Moors and other Low Vegetation Areas	27
	The Ross Moors	27
	Loophead Moors	51
4	Rocky, Stony and Sandy Beaches	61
	Ross Beach	61
	Rhynvella Beach	71
5	Waysides, Verges, Hedgerows and Drains	79
6	The Inspired Artworks	123
Bibliography		142
Acknowledgments		143
Index		144
Poetry - Garden of Entangled Freedom		9
- On a Stony Beach		62
- Freedom Blossoms		79
- Christmas Day - Kilballyowen - Walk through the Snow		81
- Tunes of the Breeze		94
- Sweet Flowers of Summer		111
- Rage on New Years Day		121
- Old Man on the Bench		141

Dedicated to:

My Parents
Mai & P.J. Magner

My Husband
Peter

My Sons
Fergal, Robert & James

For your inspiration, encouragement & kindness

FOREWORD - *by Stephen Ward*

The Wild Flowers of Loophead tells of a family, of a daughter - Carmel, her mother and father and family who have farmed at the Bridges of Ross for ten generations or more; of a mother - the very same Carmel, and her youngest son, James, who between them developed a deep interest in the flowers of this Atlantic headland and set about describing and recording them.

Carmel's account is more than a flower book. She captures the moods of headland and ocean in prose, photos, poetry and palette. Wild Carrot - a decadent lace-like plant with drooping green feathery bracts she considers 'a testament to the glory of nature'.

The peaks and troughs of grass and heath on the Loophead moors have been sculpted by the wind; here the waterlogged cliff-top with Sea Aster and luxurious large tussocks of Thrift is reminiscent of saltmarsh. Carmel's love of colour and place is brought to life as she describes the honey-scent of Bell Heather and Ling blooming around the lighthouse and at Ross, where the blue heads of Sheep's-bit *'pull down the blue sky and pull up the Atlantic'* an ever present giddying drop below.

She takes joy from the Peninsula's tall hedgerows with their Honeysckle and differing flowers on the sunny and shady sides and their solitude and fresh breezes. In Spring, Primroses flower at every crossroads, in the ditches and on the muddy vertical cliff sides at Ross; she recalls hair-raising climbs as a child to collect them. Later Purple Loosestrife bedecks the ditches and the hedgerows hum with flies, bees, butterflies and birds.

The possibility of foraging for vegetables are not overlooked; Rock Samphire, Sea Beet, Sea Rocket, Scurvy Grass are all good sources of vitamin C. Furze was used to get the oven hot for baking bread, also for fodder; Red Clover enriches the pasture for the cattle.

Herbal remedies aplenty are presented; Navelwort to suppress bleeding; Curly Dock to soothe Nettle stings, Herb Robert and Angelica for toothache, Meadow sweet as nature's aspirin; Fleabane - burnt to rid house of fleas.

Carmel's joy in her surroundings is not confined to Spring and Summer. On Christmas Day at Kilballyowen she recalls a
'Walk through the Snow':
'Unique in my lifetime and my mother's nine decades.'

*'The now lifeless umbels and florets of Summer's blossoms
delicately spun in Winter's most decadent purest lace.'*

Stephen Ward,
Ballyvaughan,
Co. Clare

Cat's-ear	 Common Centaury	 Elecampane	 Common Mallow
 Honeysuckle		 Scarlet Pimpernel	 English Stonecrop
 Kidney Vetch	Babington's Leek	 Eyebright	 Greater Willowherb

FOREWORD - *by Paul R. Green*

I first visited Ireland in 1988 and fell in love with the country. I came over for the Botanical Society of the British Isles(BSBI) to do voluntary field survey work in Counties Galway and Waterford. Despite my love of Ireland it was another nine years before I was to return. Again I was asked by the BSBI to help record for a new atlas of the plants of Britain and Ireland, mostly in Co. Waterford in 1997/98 and a very rapid three week survey over the whole of Co. Cork in 1999. I continued to visit Co. Waterford several times each year to record the flowers which culminated in *'The Flora of Co. Waterford'* in 2008. By this time I had been living in Ireland for two years at New Ross, Co. Wexford.

'The Wild Flowers of Loophead' is the study of the plants over a number of years of this remote rugged beautiful headland stretching into the vast expanse of the Atlantic Ocean. The windswept landscape is almost tree free and what species do grow here have to cope with extreme weather conditions. This beautiful part of Co. Clare has been largely ignored by botanists as they are attracted to the vast botanically rich limestone of the Burren.

There is much to discover in this book. Common Centaury flowers close up in the early evening and research at Cork Institute of Technology has shown that extracts from Elecampane kill MRSA, and a broad range of other bacteria.

Following the walks described in this book, on a fine day there are wonderful views to be had of the north Kerry coastline with Brandon Mountain standing proud in the distance and the loose stone walls make a backdrop for the flowers. The open peaty moors are a tapestry of wild flowers keeping the botanist intoxicated.

The wild flowers of Loophead add colour over much of the year with Thrift pink covered cliffs and ditches and later in the year the bushes of Fuchsia, rich red and purple dangling flowers and large swathes of orange of Montbretia. On a warm sunny day the air is perfumed with coconut from the flowers of Gorse(Furze).

This book will help you escape the busy everyday life and give you a chance to enjoy nature's wonders while enjoying the solitude of Loophead.

Paul R. Green
Ballycullane,
Co. Wexford

Wild Carrot

Sea Campion

Thrift

Montbretia

Irish Marsh Orchid

Burnet Rose

Sheep's-bit

Sea Aster

Wild Thyme

English Stonecrop

Garden of Entangled Freedom

Where the wild rush doth
pick its moisture rich niche
on the edge of the drain by the road,
where there its slick slender growth,
criss cross and encroach
without care, or permission sought.

Below at its base, a luscious embrace
of species of blade laden grasses,
and the Vetch flowers that flourish
with their tendrils entwined,
we find, paired leaves and delicate florets.

As all growth must fasten, set root
on the ground, this low density
has no order or pattern,
but a simple desire to gain light and grow higher
and survive in this tangled wild garden.

Each one has its merit,
and entitlement to inhabit
this garden by the side of the road,
the Trefoils are edgy, with their Christian solidarity,
whilst the Bird's-foot lights up the whole world.

The taller plants can, at once entrance,
with spikes and clusters a plenty:
Purple Loosestrife's surprise in spikes delight,
Fleabane's golden florets in fringe prevail,
while pastel shades of Carrot remain pale.

The Spirit of Freedom inhabits this place,
a ruleless, boundless Kingdom,
where weak may falter and strong invade,
where powerful plants in Winter fade,
where seeds blew in and set up home,
or by bird or fly, continue to roam.

(2012)

The exquisitely formed umbels of the **Wild Carrot** proudly exhibit on the moors at the Bridges of Ross.

Chapter 1 - Introduction

Stretching its ancient rugged Namurian Geological formation far into the vast expanse of the Atlantic Ocean, the Loophead Peninsula is at once exposed, isolated, raw and startlingly beautiful. The atmospheric moods of the ocean wield a powerful influence on the surrounding lands, its mood turning often as rapid as its strong fast-moving ocean currents. It brings with it an airflow that is often drenched in saline droplets, that sometimes roars ashore in gale force storm, or that surrounds us in a refreshing, warming crispy breeze. Whatever the mood, whatever its colour, the Atlantic Ocean provides a backdrop of continuous natural movement, to everything that moves, stands still or just simply exists on the Peninsula lands.

My ancestral home has stood on the Peninsula for over three hundred years, it being the oldest house in Ross and the last remaining domicile of the old townland. My exposure to the wild and raw beauty at Loophead has therefore existed since birth. This exposure is not only visual, atmospheric, elemental, it is also spiritual and it brings with it the constant unique natural sounds that emanate from a vast volume of water that has reached its destination, lashing, rippling, pounding, dragging, rarely silent. It brings with it the lively screeches of the Ocean Gulls, the faultless, flawless, synchronized gliding and diving of Fulmars, Herring Gulls and Gannets, and their often energizing uproarious carry-on, that fills the senses with the grandeur of nature's never-ending festivities.

It is therefore against this mesmerizing backdrop, that I set out to research my project on wild flowers. Almost always accompanied by James my young son, who brings bubbly conversation, un-rivalled joy and a great sense of comradeship to the field, his simple enjoyment and comments fill treasured moments, and I never feel isolated in his warming affectionate company. It was James too, who purchased the first book which led to our adventure of identification of the wild Flowers of Loophead, his appetite for natural knowledge insatiable.

And so our research has led us through furze and fen, moor and cliff, drain and hedgerow, shore and wayside as we set out with pen and paper, camera, magnifying glass and books in our quest to research and record the wild flora of Loophead. This work began in earnest in early Summer 2007, and still continues, with an open register, ready to add another species. Through the years, we continued to return to old sites, to watch the behaviour of our wild flowers, to determine their flowering times and seek linkage to particular weather patterns, and secretly to be inspired and enthralled anew by their delicate beauty, their resourceful approach towards survival and their Spirit of Freedom.

Artistically, I am imbued with the radiance and irreverence, of that wild freedom. My works are expressionist and uncontrolled, full of raw energy, vigour and tangled detail. There is no need to state here what inspires this work, as the answer can be found in the previous paragraphs. People too seek this sense of simple freedom. Meeting people through my regular exhibitions, I often see an inner Spirit trying to break free from the controlled Society we live in. There is a quest for simplicity, realignment with nature's activities and creations. The Wild Flowers of Loophead, driven by the open windy territory provide a joyous dance, a welcoming bow, a splash of delightful colour, a unique individualism. Our senses have been filled with their beauty and adoptive natural antics.

This book, seeks to present the reader with each flower recorded and described in one of its common habitats. Each chapter describes a habitat, for example the Rocky and Stony Shores, the Open Peaty and Tufted Moors, The Waysides, Verges, Hedgerows and Drains, because many of the plants recorded are particular to specific

INTRODUCTION

habitats, that contain the appropriate soils, moisture, sun exposure and salt levels for flourishing.

The moors around Loophead Lighthouse are vast and exposed and provide for at least a full day of walking to explore their topography and floral footprint. The particular flowers one are likely to meet depends on the timing of the trip, but an early- mid May trip is a must to catch the colourful display of the Sea Pinks (Thrift). To view the flush of Irish Marsh Orchids, requires an early June trip, as these short lasting flowers will whither quickly. Later in June the intense flowering colour of the Wild Thyme which clumps itself here and there on the thinner soil, draws one into its powerful aura. Visiting in August, the wonderful Sea Aster provides a very handsome display.

A focal historical point of these moors is Loophead Lighthouse, which at 23 metres tall, can be seen from any part of the moors, providing guidance to the natural explorer and in times past guidance to the fishermen and shipping companies that entered the Shannon Estuary.
The long since silenced foghorn used to alert shipping to poor visible conditions nearing shore, as it bellowed its deep boom across the Peninsula and out to sea, still remains in my ears as a unique Peninsula sound.

A blossoming breeze of mystic romance pervades the air at Loophead as the legendary fable of Diarmuid and Grainne unfolds itself in the giant leap from the moors on to Diarmuid's and Grainne's rock a tall stack just 40 feet off shore that sits North West of the Lighthouse and can be seen from the moors. So too do the difficult to locate 'Hanging Gardens' provide a sense of intrigue, plateaus and natural ledges used by the Landlord to entertain guests in open air picnics during Summer months.

There is the evidence of the requirement for territorial protection on these moors, which presents in the large stone 'EIRE' signage used to declare ownership of territory together with the now dilapidated 'Coastguard Station' located on the moors and used to spot and report threats from the ocean during the war time.

On the much smaller, but no less important moor top at Ross, which

The Ocean and its high flying inhabitants provide a continuous drama, whilst nestled in the soft springy moors, a varied cache of tiny wild flowers waiting to be appreciated.

Fresh air permeates every nook and cranny, whilst the Summer breezes bow the long linear leaves of the Montbretia offering the visitor a natural welcome to the area.

INTRODUCTION

The horizontal lines of a flat and tree less landscape draws your undivided attention to the wild and colourful hedgerows in peak season.

The Purple Loosestrife shares flowering space with the sweetly aromatic Meadowsweet in this densely populated hedgerow that thrives organically and labour free.

also covers the 'Ross Formation' the title assigned to the significant Geological Sandstone and Shale Namurian Basin, continuously visited by Universities around the world, who produce scholarly papers, reports and websites on their findings, one finds the simply exquisite and delicate Common Centaury, from late June. In late May into June, one finds gorgeous mat-forming and ground hugging English Stonecrop, together with Wild Thyme, and the fluffy blue flower heads of Sheep's - bit which diagonally grow out of their basal rosettes on the low mud-stone ditches. Visiting the moor tops at Ross from mid-late July, one is likely to encounter a fabulous display of Ling and a 'nesting' of bird watchers perched beside the Bridges of Ross, facing to the ocean, clad in gear that keeps out the breeze and mist, while they patiently await day after day from early morning, the Autumnal migration of otherwise unseen birds. According to the blogging bird watchers who visit this site, together with Clare Bird Watching, the birds fly very close to the coast at this location, and the species include Fea's Petrel, all the Shearwaters and Skuas, Kittiwakes, Arctic Terns, Whimbrel, Sabine's Gull, Guillemot, Puffins, Shags, Fulmars, and lots of Gannets. These bird watchers are not folk who conceal their excitement, when a rare bird flies past, and can in themselves provide the moor walker with an uplifting sense of wonder. The bird watchers congregate here from all corners of Ireland and Europe.

Not to be outshone by the shenanigans of the Loophead moors, the Ross moors provided the work base to the crew and stars of 'Ryan's Daughter', notably Sarah Miles and John Mills, for three months during the wild Winter of 1968/69, as they set-up a film base and land tracking to Ross Point to film a stormy scene in the film under the directorship of the legendary David Lean.

Taking ones exploration to the rocky, stony and sandy shores of both Ross and Rhynvella, one finds a unique habitat, that supports a different variation of wild flora. This is the home of the Sea Mayweed, a ferny-leaved large daisy-like flower that delivers a mustard and white colouring and a friendly demeanour. This is also the home of the Rock Sea Spurrey, Bittersweet, Oraches, Sea Beet, Rock Samphire, Common Scurvy Grass, Sea Rocket and a host of other wild flowers that are common to several habitats. In the more

Stunningly and perfectly formed yet dwarfed Buck's horn Plantain on bare peat at Loophead moors.

salt marshy conditions especially at Ross Beach, one finds the Sea Milkwort, Sea Club Rush, and Reeds. These beaches are species-rich habitats with abundant Lichens - the Orange Lichen and the Sea Ivory making particularly striking displays. Seaweeds, such as the Carrageen Moss, Channel Wrack, Bladder Wrack, Spiral Wrack, Egg Wrack, Dilisk, Sea Grass, Sea Lettuce, Ribbon Weed, and Tangle and Sugar Kelp grow in the Intertidal Zone or are washed up in storms and high tides. In the sandy gravels, are the abandoned shells of Limpets, Mussels, Toothed Topshell, Purple Topshell, Painted Topshell, Dog Whelks, and Flat Periwinkles.

INTRODUCTION

Perhaps it is the Peninsula's tall hedgerow and wayside vegetation that provides the greatest display of colour. From mid-July onward, these hedgerows, combining a feast of Meadowsweet, Purple Loosestrife, Greater Willowherb, Montbretia, Knapweed, Creeping, Marsh and Spear Thistles, Vetches, Fleabanes and St. Johns-wort and delivering a bounty of wild flora, entangled yet free that thrill the senses. The peaceful inner roads, like those at Rehy, Kilballyowen and Ross present the explorer with a sense of quiet solitude together with fresh Peninsula breezes, open country treeless views and a horizontal landscape of low ditches, green fields and the fluttering and buzzing of butterflies and bees generating an atmospheric masterpiece.

This book aims to present the rich and often overlooked floral diversity of Loophead. As aforementioned, the reasons for visiting Loophead are manifold, Geology, Birds, Whale & Dolphin Watching, Wave Action, Fresh Ocean Air, Rare Topography, Underwater Biodiversity, Historical Monuments and Wild Flora including Lichens, and Seaweeds. Loophead and its environs is a place apart and a place unique. It is of paramount importance that the visitor, treats its natural bounty with respect and appreciation. This place is a sanctuary for those who have left, but return time and again to be refreshed, relaxed and reunited with nature. It is a place of intrigue for first time visitors, who could not possibly experience its natural supremacy in a short singular trip. Loophead calls you back time and again, to be free, be immersed, be mesmerized.

Through parking and walking, one can experience at first hand the treasures of Loophead. I have incorporated an illustrated Botanical Glossary of terms used within the subsequent chapters to assist the newcomer to wild flora. This book aims to be simple and concise in its presentation of the flora, where possible building a personality around each flower, because each flower is an ultimate individual. Each flower is photographed in its natural habitat at Loophead and no photo enhancements have taken place, allowing the viewer to easily identify the flowers in the field.

A wonderful journey unfolds.

WESTERN LOOPHEAD PENINSULA

INTRODUCTION

Map Legend:
- Main Road R487
- Quiet Inner Roads - Suit Walking & Cycling
- Country Lanes - Walking

IRELAND — Western Loophead Peninsula

CO. CLARE — Western Loophead Peninsula

ATLANTIC OCEAN

SHANNON ESTUARY

Locations and features:
- Knocknagarhoon
- Trusklieve
- Kilkee
- Tullig Point
- Tullig
- Cross Village — Parking/Refreshments, Rich Floral Hedgerows nearby
- Ross Moors - Flora, Western/Eastern Track, Bridge of Ross/Geology, Care! Precipitous Cliffs!, Bird Watching, Parking/Fishing Nearby
- Ross
- Kilbaha Kiltrellig
- R487
- Kilballyowen - Rehy
- Carrigaholt
- Ross Rocky & Stony Beach/Flora/Seaweeds/Lichens
- Fodera - Elevated Ocean Views
- Church of the Little Ark Moneen
- Kilclogher - Rehy
- Loophead Moors Flora, Loophead Lighthouse, Diarmuid & Grainne's R., Whale & Dolphin Watch, Care! Precipitous Cliffs!, Birds/Ocean, Exhibition Centre/Parking, Eire Sign/Coastguard
- Kilbaha — Sea front Restaurants, Pier & Rocky Shore, Sculptures, Walking/Parking
- Rhynvella Beach Flora, Sandy & Rocky Shore, Scenic views across Shannon River/Rehy Hill, Safe Bathing/Walking, Roadside Parking

Chapter 2: Getting Started

Entering the normally quiet and peaceful Peninsula roads, one needs to realize the importance of not rushing to a final destination. Slow down. All roads to Loophead have an Easterly orientation, there is no further West. Loophead is a full stop. One cannot expect to experience its fulsome and varied natural treasure, if one is committed to a short time frame, a singular reason for visiting, arriving and departing at high speed or inappropriately prepared and attired for a refreshing Peninsula experience.

Depending on your visit, one can be met with the harvest buzz of its farming community, the main stayer of the local economy here. The locals are friendly and welcoming. My dad spent decades greeting visitors at the Bridges of Ross car park, scouting for exchanges of life experiences, and fulfilling the needs for local knowledge, requested by the visitor, like a self-directed 'Tourist Office'. The resulting dividend for him, is a network of friendships that extends across the world, and an International bundle of Christmas cards and hand written letters arriving to his door. The locals probably take their surrounding environment for granted, being in its presence every day. Luckily for the generally dairy farming community, who find it difficult to get away from daily milking chores, there is no need to get away, with such natural beauty and serenity in abundance and attachment to the earth, one could happily be always here. The harvesting buzz depends on the weather but normally reaches a peak by mid-June, thereafter the roads will be less busy with harvesting traffic and therefore safer for walkers and cyclists.

This book seeks to introduce the natural explorer to the wild flora of Loophead and therefore is largely written around visiting the area from March to September. Visiting Loophead during the darkened bleak days of December/January will be an eye catching, eye opening experience, should you meet the rough Spring tides, frothing, fiercesome and furiously driven waves, freshly delivered from across the Atlantic, which will be remembered on the cheeks of your exposed face for days. Refreshed and wind-swept! The hedgerows and fields too will tell their bleak story of being withered by the unforgiving salty strong winds, and will linger lifeless, until nature turns up its Springtime heat.

As a destination, Loophead delivers a number of options for flower spotting to the tourist. The first options are to head straight for the open moors at either Ross or Loophead. I personally love both these moors especially from late April onward. The Ross moors are compact but richly populated with a wide variety of normally small delicate flora. The more extensive Loophead moors have taller vegetation in places, are grassier and one has to spread around every corner of the moors to gain a good understanding of its floral footprint. For road ramblers, Loophead is a mecca of quite narrow roads. The open flat landscape provides commanding country views. Tall trees do not exist here, and the Whitethorn, Blackthorn, and Elder that inhabit some of the boundary ditches are stunted by the South Westerly winds. Walking on the inner roads of the Peninsula, one meets with interesting plant behavioural patterns. At one side of the road facing the sun, live plants which enjoy sunshine, while at the other side of the road, the plants which enjoy shade. This makes it important for the flower spotter to view both sides of each narrow road. This chapter also aims to provide the novice with simple leaf and flower head diagrams to assist in understanding Botanical terminology used in the book.

Natural Exploration is a personal adventure and I do not plan to feed the reader with too much hand-held insight, but enough to conquer the curiosity, and provide a starting point. Therefore I will describe two routes that the visitor can use and earlier a map showing all the little inner roads that will expose your senses.

ROUTE 1 - ROSS-KILTRELLIG LOOPED ROUTE
Distance approx 8.5km - Time required approx 2.5 hours
See Map - Ross Area - 5, 11, 12, 14, 1, 4

Amongst the flora - peace and serenity prosper - James at Ross early May.

Migrating birds provide natural entertainment - bird-watchers at Ross

One could spend much longer on this looped walk, as there are many side shows that could be added to this walk.

Western Loophead Region - Ross Area

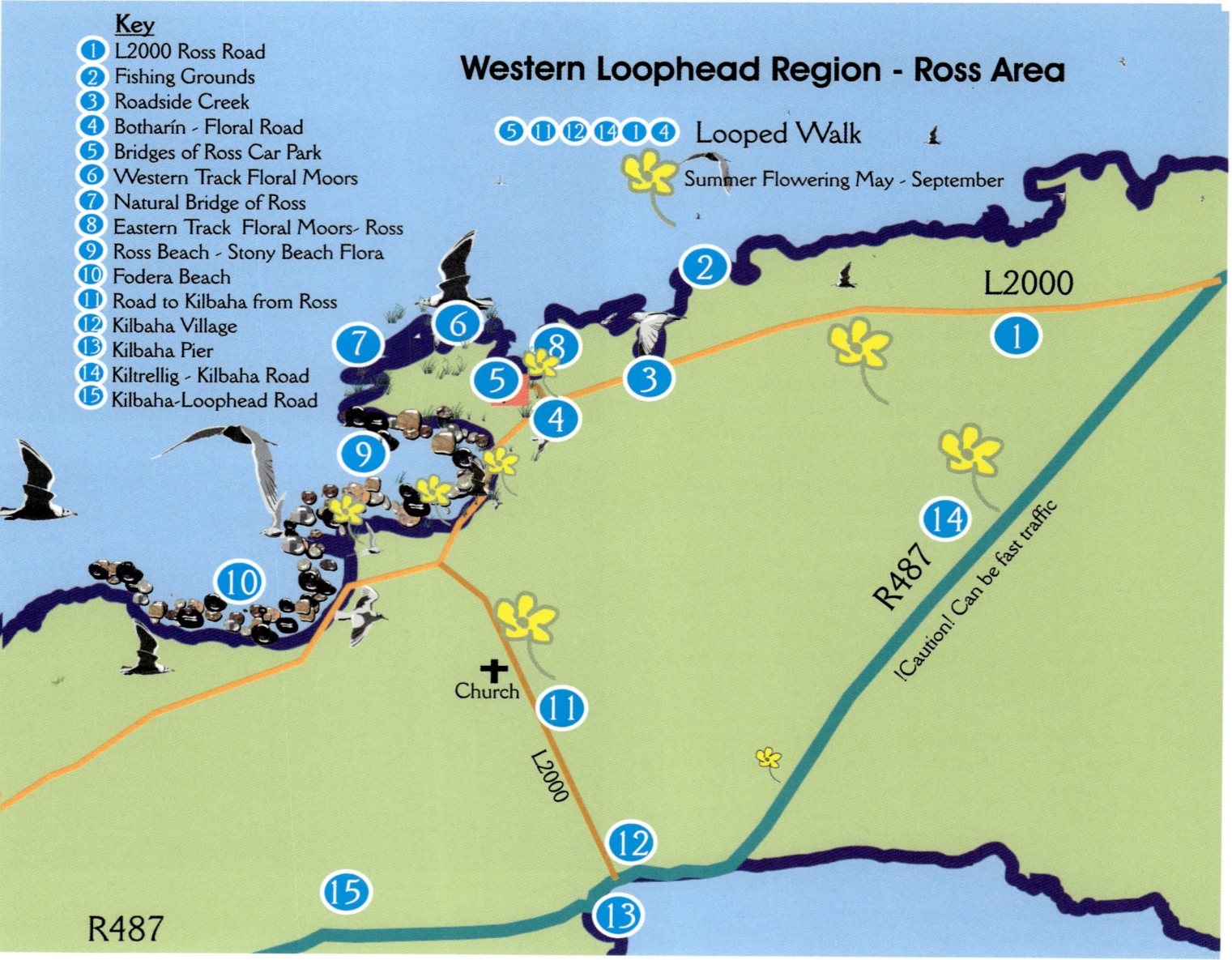

Key
1. L2000 Ross Road
2. Fishing Grounds
3. Roadside Creek
4. Botharín - Floral Road
5. Bridges of Ross Car Park
6. Western Track Floral Moors
7. Natural Bridge of Ross
8. Eastern Track Floral Moors- Ross
9. Ross Beach - Stony Beach Flora
10. Fodera Beach
11. Road to Kilbaha from Ross
12. Kilbaha Village
13. Kilbaha Pier
14. Kiltrellig - Kilbaha Road
15. Kilbaha-Loophead Road

⑤ ⑪ ⑫ ⑭ ① ④ Looped Walk

Summer Flowering May - September

L2000

R487 ¡Caution! Can be fast traffic

Church

R487

GETTING STARTED

Park your car at the Bridges of Ross car park. You may decide to take in these moors at the start of your walk. Take the little botharín back to the main road and take right, heading towards Ross Beach. You may pass the beach or take a look at its inner vegetation. On the outside you will encounter Sea Mayweed, Perennial Sow Thistle, Hedge Bindweed, Silverweed, Curled Dock. Passing the beach and moving toward the next cross roads junction, take left toward the Church of the Little Ark and Community Centre. The road along here has been raised above the bog/fen surrounding it. In late July/August, you will be treated to a feast of the damp bog loving Purple Loosestrife, as it spreads itself across large areas of fen off-road. The hedgerows here are low and grassy and not as colourful as those of the Kiltrellig Road. However you will find plants like Meadowsweet, Cat's -ear, and Silverweed along this stretch. It is worth taking the detour into the Church of the Little Ark in Moneen, to view the Little Ark that was constructed in landlord times to allow Mass be celebrated on 'No Man's Land'- beside the sea shore at Kilbaha. Full historical details can be found at the Church. Continuing on the L2000 towards Kilbaha village, one encounters a refreshing breezy openness as you near the first major bay of the Shannon River, Kilbaha Bay, a relatively sheltered gently rounded stony and rocky bay with a pier area to the west of the bay. Here one can linger on the beach top or at the local restaurants that flank it with their outdoor seating and local produce menus to entice your taste buds.

The next part of your walk will be on the R487, a busier route flanking the shoreline until it curves you around towards the townland of Kiltrellig. On a fine day, there are particularly nice views of the North Kerry coastline with the Brandon Mountains looming in the distance. As the crow flies, the Kerry shoreline is but fourteen kilometers away from here. Kiltrellig provides a wonderful display of flowers such as the Montbretia, Greater Willowherb, Purple Loosestrife, Meadowsweet, Clovers and earlier in the season, Lesser Celandine, Ragged Robin, Early Purple and Marsh Orchids, Cuckoo Flower, Self Heal, Trailing Tormentil, and Silverweed. The road is long and straight and leads you to the junction at Anvil Farm, where you take left on the

The loose stone ditches at Ross provide a muted background for its floral displays.

L2000 back on the Ross Road.

On the Ross Road, you will soon meet the now rare Marsh Mallow growing out of the drains not far into your Westerly trip. This plant has soft grey green densely hairy leaves, with large soft lavender coloured flower heads with deeper coloured centers. This is the only location of this plant that I have found in the area, and it is rare countrywide.

Nearing the top of Ross hill, one sees the wonderful vista of both the Atlantic Ocean and the Shannon River, as the Peninsula narrows from north to south. On a fine day, the sky is luminous and bears its luminosity on the ocean's surface. This radiance fulfils the being, which together with the swishing breezes amongst the long linear leaves of the Montbretia leaves the being utterly refreshed. You will also pass the narrow roadside Creek at Ross, and as you near the little botharín that delivers you back to your car, remember to check it on both sides for the tiny, unusual and interesting flora that inhabit the botharín ditches.

Western Loophead Region - Kilballyowen-Rhynvella Loop

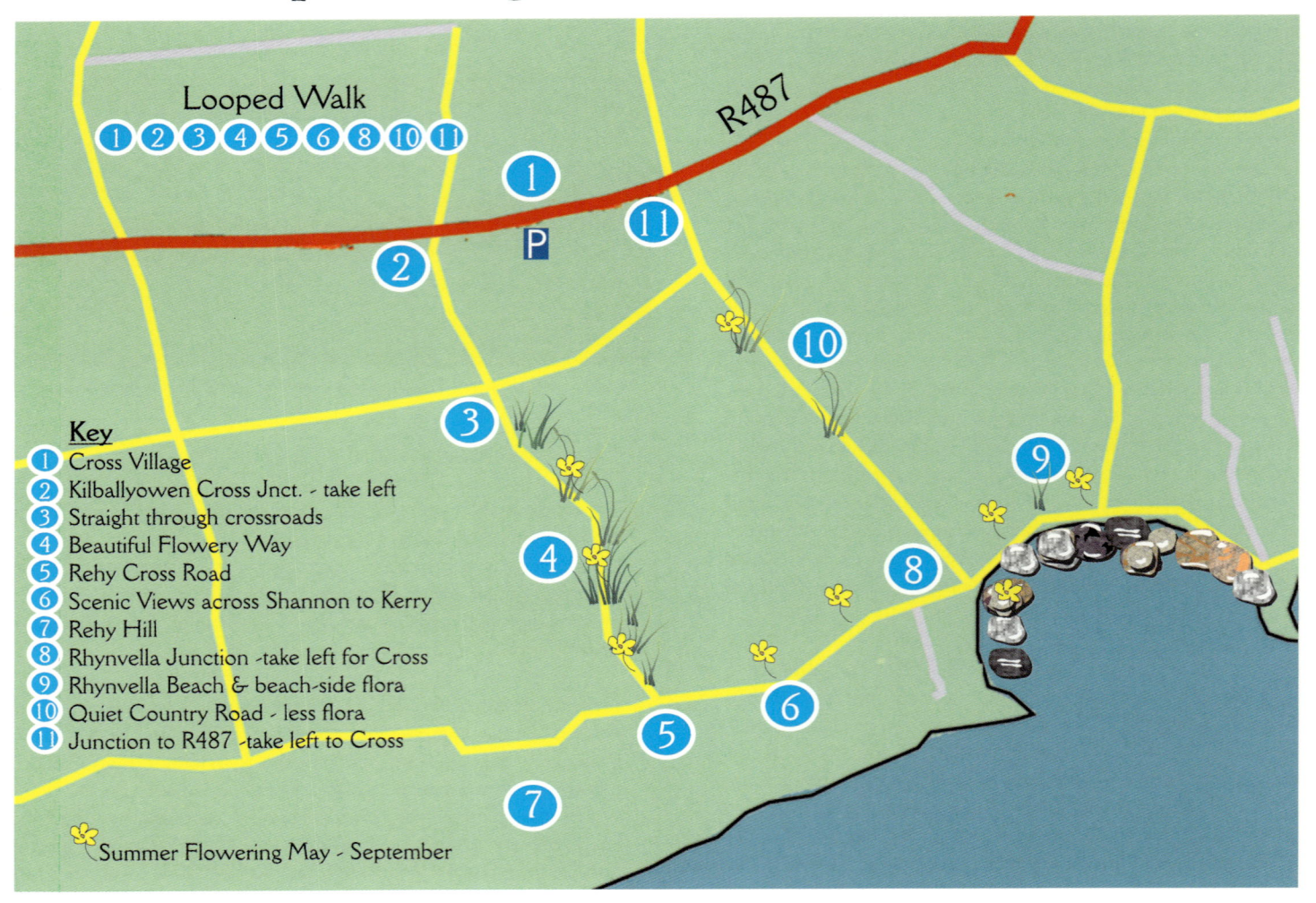

Looped Walk
① ② ③ ④ ⑤ ⑥ ⑧ ⑩ ⑪

R487

Key
1. Cross Village
2. Kilballyowen Cross Jnct. - take left
3. Straight through crossroads
4. Beautiful Flowery Way
5. Rehy Cross Road
6. Scenic Views across Shannon to Kerry
7. Rehy Hill
8. Rhynvella Junction - take left for Cross
9. Rhynvella Beach & beach-side flora
10. Quiet Country Road - less flora
11. Junction to R487 - take left to Cross

Summer Flowering May - September

ROUTE 2 - CROSS-KILBALLYOWEN-RHYNVELLA-CROSS
Distance approx. 6.7km - Time required approx. 1.5-2 hours
See Map - Kilballyowen-Rhynvella Loop - 1,2,3,4,5,6,8,10,11

This walking route is one of the most scenic, colourful and species rich walks of the high flowering season from mid July. In addition, there is little vehicular traffic on this route, which greatly adds to its enjoyment.

Park your car in Cross Village and head West towards Loophead. A short distance West of the village, take the first left junction, heading South. You will pass the Naomh Eoin football pitch on your right. There are lovely displays of Montbretia, Purple Loosestrife, Meadowsweet, Greater Willowherb and many more. There is a busy hive of insect activity partaking and there is normally a swishing Summer breeze. The horizontal landscape is peaked by Rehy Hill at a height of 116m in the centre distance. The hedgerows are tall, and are Bramble rich, and from August deliver a bountiful harvest of blackberries. At point 5, on the map take left at the Rehy Junction heading East. Babington's Leek has a small population on this road, normally flowering from June. This road leads to Rhynvella Beach. Before you turn, you will encounter a lovely display of Fuchsia if you look West at this junction. A little into your Eastern trip, you will begin to see the Shannon Estuary unfold with the undulating Kerry coastline just approximately three kilometres away. This is a picturesque view, and changes mood and colour with the sky and tide. At point 8, you may return Northwards on your looped walk, but I highly recommend that you continue the short distance to Rhynvella Beach. Here you can check the road/waysides at both sides of the road. My favourite flower, in this area is the Wild Carrot. Inside the beach are the flowers covered in the Rocky and Stony Shores chapter of this book. Rhynvella Beach also provides safe bathing and a somewhat sandy shore, depending on tide level. If you have taken this detour, head back to point 8, taking North, in a more uphill route, that is little trafficked, less colourful, than its parallel comrade. This will lead you back to Cross Village, when you take left at point 11.

Babington's Leek salutes a blue sky near Rhynvella (between points 5 &8)

CHERISH AND FLOURISH!

The place names used in this book may differ somewhat from those on road signage or other maps. The spellings I have used are those learned during my national school years. The following spelling variations may occur:

Fodera	Fodry	
Rhynvella	Rinevella	
Cloughaunsavaune	Cloghaunsavaun	Clohansevan

The floral environment at Loophead is delicate and fragile, and requests your genuine respect.

All flora described in this book may be viewed from publicly accessible viewpoints, on moors, beaches, waysides, verges, hedgerows and drains.

Take care and keep yourself and your children safe especially on cliff/moor tops. Stay well away from the verge.

Leave no un-welcome trace, and just take your memories and photographs.

Slow down.

Enjoy your adventure

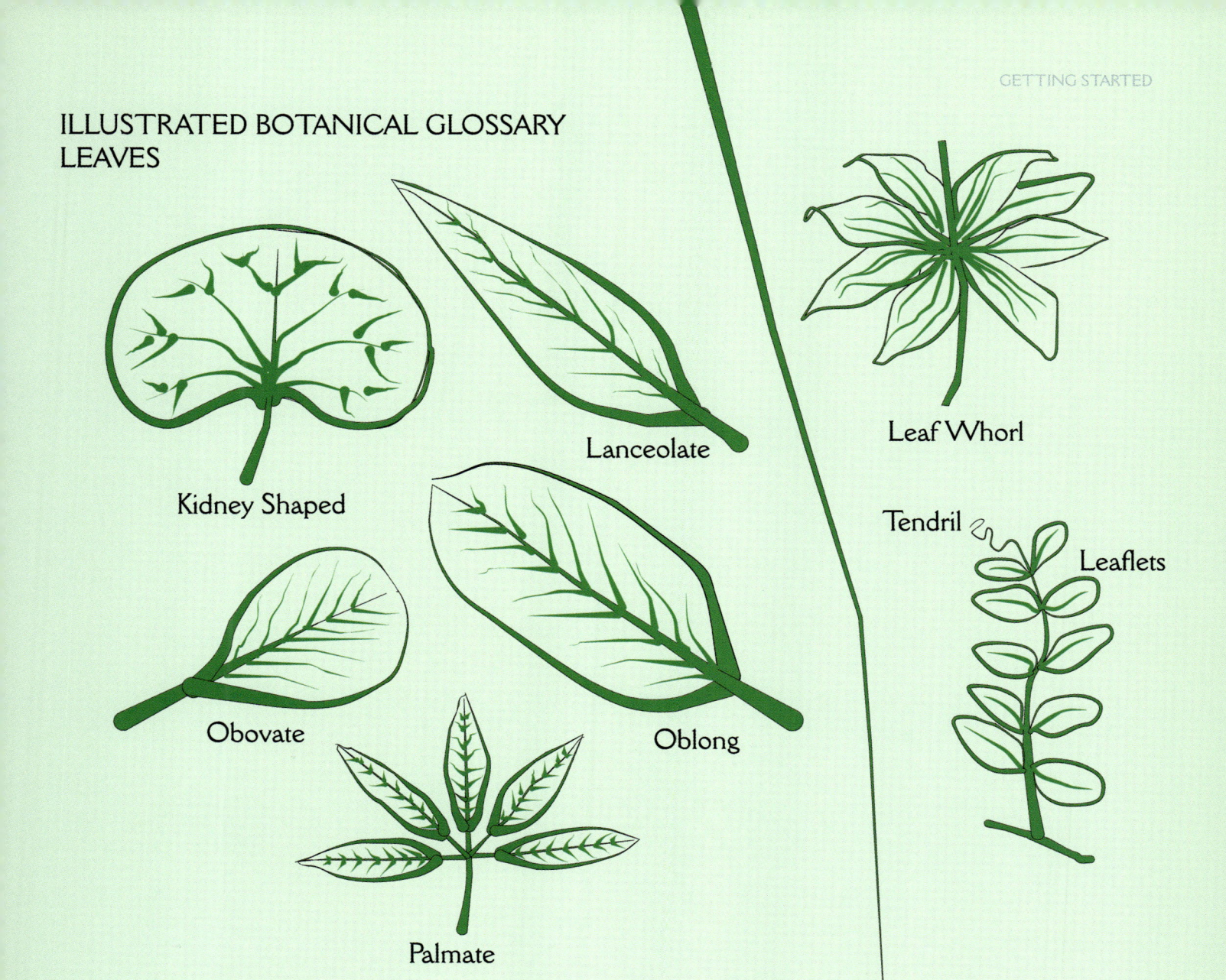

ILLUSTRATED BOTANICAL GLOSSARY
LEAVES

Kidney Shaped

Lanceolate

Obovate

Oblong

Palmate

Leaf Whorl

Tendril

Leaflets

GETTING STARTED

23

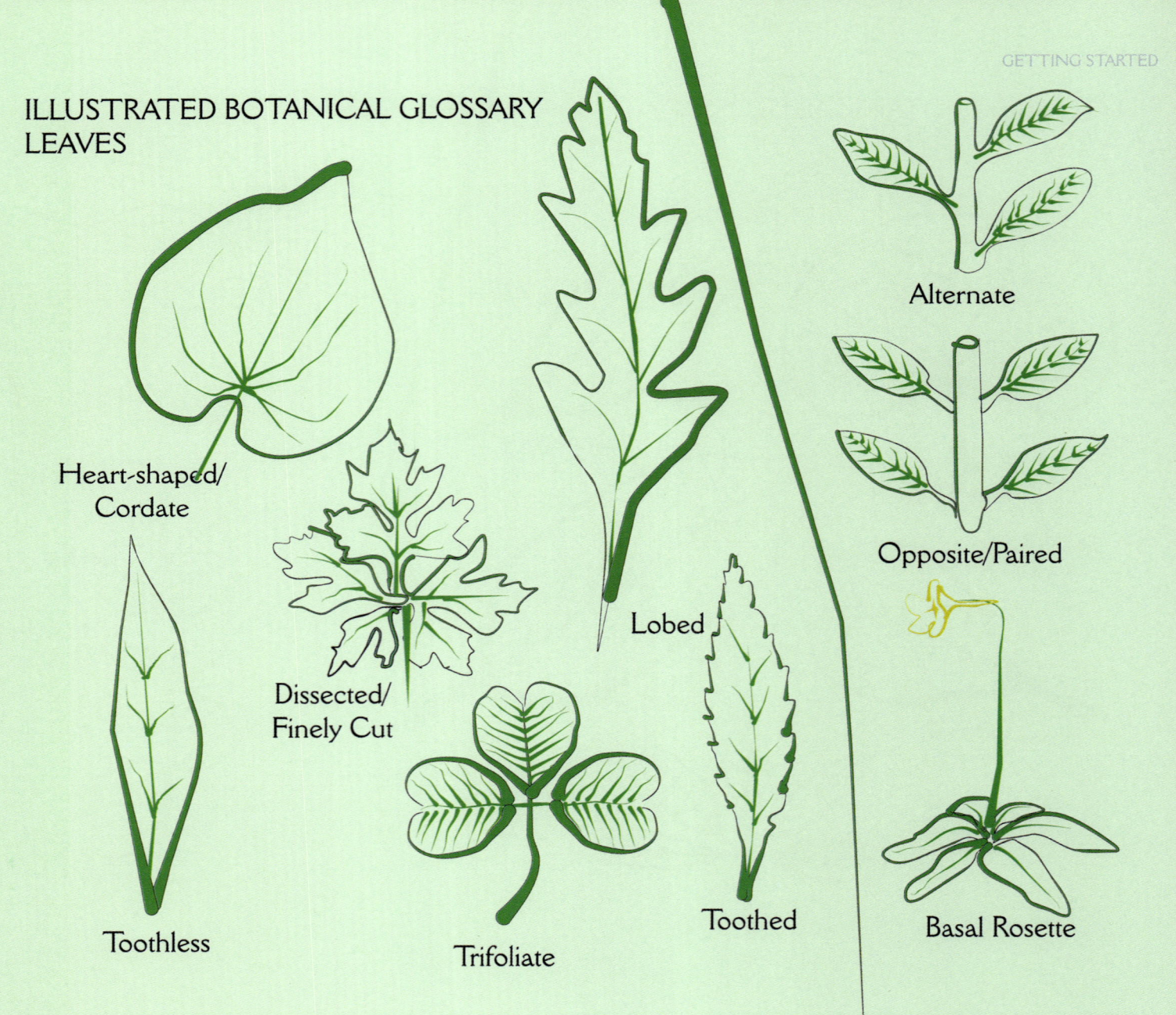

ILLUSTRATED BOTANICAL GLOSSARY
LEAVES

Heart-shaped/Cordate

Dissected/Finely Cut

Lobed

Alternate

Opposite/Paired

Toothless

Trifoliate

Toothed

Basal Rosette

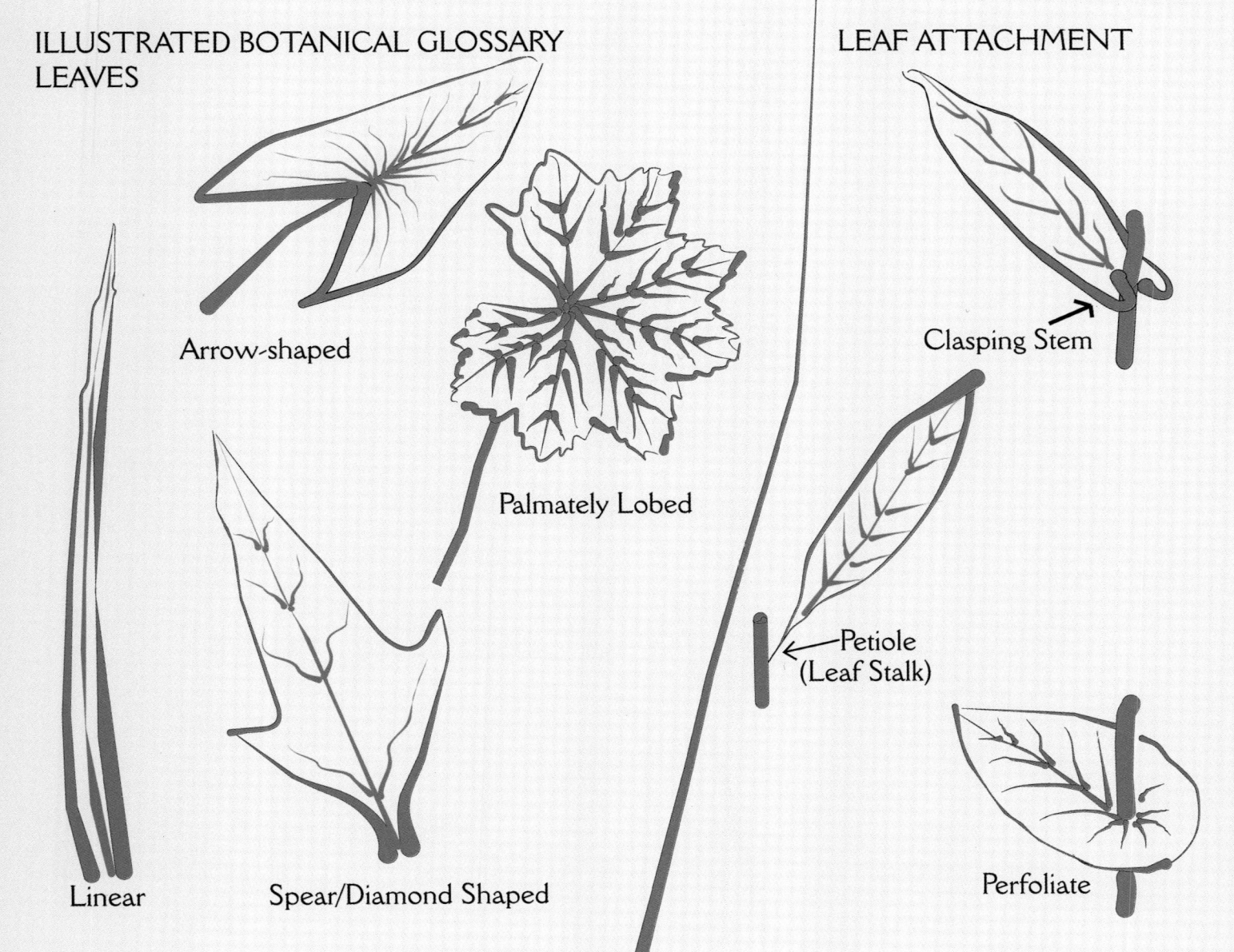

ILLUSTRATED BOTANICAL GLOSSARY
LEAVES

Arrow-shaped

Palmately Lobed

Linear

Spear/Diamond Shaped

LEAF ATTACHMENT

GETTING STARTED

Clasping Stem

Petiole (Leaf Stalk)

Perfoliate

25

ILLUSTRATED BOTANICAL GLOSSARY | SAMPLE FLOWER STRUCTURES

Corymb
A flower head where the outer flower stalks are longer than the central flower stalks so the flowers are in a flat top cluster.

Umbel
The flower stalks rise from one point at the top of the stem, and the flowers appear flat and clustered on top.

Raceme
A raceme is a spiked flower head where each flower on the spike has a separate stalk. The bottom flower opens first, and then each flower opens in sequence towards the top, and the spike can continue to grow upwards.

Spike
A spile is a flower head that has no stalks to the individual flowers on the spike.

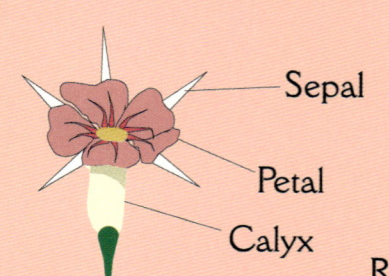

Sepal

Petal

Calyx

Ray Floret

Disc Floret

Chapter 3 - Open Peaty Moors & Other Low Vegetation Areas

THE ROSS MOORS

The combination of fresh soft winds, blue skies, and a textured tapestry of tiny wild flowers at ones feet is as intoxicating as it is real. The peaty moors at Loophead and at the Bridges of Ross, can easily be overlooked as one strives towards the cliff faces and the breaking waves and the call of the ocean birds. However, to bypass and ignore these tiny natural treasures on which you step, is to un-realize the total magic of your natural journey. The survival of these plants in a hostile natural environment is indeed heroic. Peat is almost always soggy or waterlogged and of poor vegetative quality. Yet this peat supports a knitted magical carpet of vegetation. Here one will find, the vibrant pink bell shaped flowers of Bell Heather, mingled with Ling (Heather), the most common flower of the tufted peaty moors. Their honey scented aroma attracting the bees and butterflies. Their wiry toughened evergreen form maintaining a presence on the moors right through the Winter.

It is easy to understand, how the natural explorer may lose a sense of time, in the process of admiration and investigation on these moors. A natural garden, created by combined elements of wind, soil, wings, waves and heroic willingness. Such low natural vegetation in the height of Summer, and yet one feels themselves at a height, for below at the base of the cliffs on which you're positioned moves the continuously active Atlantic Ocean. Nothing separates, beware the edge.

James on the peaty moors at Loophead with Ling (Heather)

'This is Heaven when looked down on by a Heavenly blue sky' from 'Floral Inclusion Zone near Loophead' (2006)

28

The exquisite colours, textures, and natural growth on a mud-stone ditch at Ross

In my long journey towards unscrambling the vegetation that exists in this rich natural microcosm, I am continually enthralled by the combination, and the aesthetic value of that combination. The exquisite delicacy of each element and its contribution to the total garden. Above, the fluffy blue flower heads of the Sheep's-bit, pulls down the blue sky and pulls up the Atlantic. The spent Thrift, being resurrected by the deeper pink of the Wild Thyme, whilst the Ling, and the soft grey-green Lichen (Sea Ivory) provoke a sense of intricate detail.

There is a network of rooting systems inter-mingling the crevices of the 'as you find it' mud embedded stones. This picture for me, tells the best story of nature, the unplanned and harmonic get together, and the fulfilling excitement in visualizing this. For the natural explorer to just focus on plant identification, for example, and not see the bigger picture, would be, in my opinion missing the whole point of the wilderness.

OPEN PEATY MOORS AND OTHER LOW VEGETATION AREAS

Sheep's-bit (*Jasione montana*) at Ross

English Stonecrop before flowering Season

English Stonecrop (*Sedum anglicum*) in full bloom in late June

In my near fifty years living at and frequenting Loophead, this blue flower has always beckoned my attention, maybe because it is blue, maybe because it is rare and unseen elsewhere in my travels. So I have made special journeys to the little botharín leading to the Bridges of Ross, just to connect with Sheep's-bit, a coastline plant which grows on dry low grassland, cliffs, heaths and dunes. Flowering from April to September, Sheep's-bit grows rampantly on dry peaty ditches at the Bridges of Ross, on the eastern track from the car park, and to a lesser degree on the road to Loophead. A member of the Bellflower Family, it has a rosette of downy basal leaves, with a dense rounded flower head at the end of each stem, and should not be confused with Devil's-bit, which is normally a tall branched blue flowered plant with a strong downy stem and oblong leaves, but which grows much lower on the moor tops at Ross.

Another exceptional plant of the bare mud or low vegetation ditches is the English Stonecrop. Forming itself around the shape of its location, when one initially comes upon this plant in perhaps March time, it looks like tightly knitted succulent red/green egg-shaped beads in a very dense mat. However, returning to see this plant months later in June, one sees a delectable showing of delicate five petalled star shaped soft pink/white flowers that simply thrill the senses. This is an evergreen plant, therefore you will always see it where it grows. The English Stonecrop at the Bridges of Ross can be mostly found on the Eastern walk from the car park on the ditches and sometimes mingled amongst the Heather on the wayside.

To survive the frequent hostilities of the strong burning salt-laden winds that frequent the Peninsula, it is probably best to be small and compact in stature, as is the case of the very lovely Common Centaury. Seeing this plant for the first time, is like the bewitching of the great and mighty by the tiny, sweet and delicate. This tiny striking five petalled pink flower with yellow stamens is common on the very low vegetation moors both at Loophead and on the moors at the Bridges of Ross. However, to find it, one has to tread carefully, with open eyes, as it barely lifts its pretty self above the vegetation surrounding it. Do not plan on viewing this flower from mid-afternoon onward, as it closes its flower head in the early evening. A member of the Gentian Family, this plant is remarkably similar to the Lesser Centaury which is normally smaller than the normally taller Common Centaury!

Common Centaury *(Centaurium erythraea)*, frequents the open moors at Ross

This narrow Western track from the Bridges of Ross car park, presents the visitor with open views of ocean sculpted rocks being crashed upon by the lively rolling waves as the Atlantic drives blindly onto its final destination to the north. To the south, the visitor can view the entire flat lands leading to the Shannon Estuary, low-lying fields bounded by low mud-stone ditches. Dropping one's eyes to the closer detail one is accompanied along this path by a myriad of tiny coastal plants, like the Common Centaury, Tormentil, Cat's-ear, Sea Pinks, Wild Thyme, Heather, Bell Heather, Sea Campion, and if you can find it, the visual feast of Wild Carrot. The Red Fescue Grass *(Festuca rubra)*, provides peaks and troughs, generated by ever-changing strong winds sculpting its particular demeanour and at the same time providing a soft springy underfoot to the visitor. The visitor will pass the impressive, layered geological formation of the remaining Bridge of Ross, and as they strive toward Ross Point, they will connect face to face with big luminous skies over the vast harrowed field of the glossy slate blue ocean at horizons end.

The Wild Carrot (*Daucus carota*) on the Ross Moors

On a sky bright July evening trip to the moors at Ross, in the Western direction from the car park, whilst I was looking for open flowered Common Centaury to photograph, (later realizing that Common Centaury closes its flowers for the day, by mid-afternoon!), I was pulled down on my knees by this magnificent Wild Carrot..........

I had not previously found Wild Carrot on the open moors at Ross, preferring the Shannon side as its regular habitat and also inhabiting a sun trap area at Ross Beach where its demeanour is totally different. Wild Carrot can grow up to a metre in height in the hedgerows and amongst tall vegetation, but this little carrot had adapted itself to its environment, growing no more than 20cm above ground level, with very sturdy rough stems and smaller, fleshier and blunter divided leaves than normally encountered. Its umbel of dense florets is also more convex than the flatter umbel that I was used to finding. The density of colour ranging from deep burgundy/pink to softer pink is spell binding. I spent magical moments quietly pouring over every delicate detail of this flower. Beyond doubt, the highlight of this evening's viewings, individual flowers, I concluded, are just as diverse and unique in their presentation as the human being!

OPEN PEATY MOORS AND OTHER LOW VEGETATION AREAS

James at Loophead with Tormentil

Tormentil (*Potentilla erecta*) is abundant at both Ross and Loophead

My son James and I first discovered Tormentil on the moor at Ross in 2007, and soon thereafter a significant abundance on the moors at Loophead. Tormentil is a tiny and highly divided leafy plant with normally a four petalled flower head - although five petals can also occur. The flowers are singular at the end of a long weak stalk.

Only growing to between 10-20cm one can find this bright yellow flower lighting up whole areas, or in just small singular clumps. In either case, to experience Tormentil on the low vegetation moor tops is to experience a ray of sunshine beaming at you from below like the re-awakening of Spring. A member of the Rose family, it can also be found in a trailing format, which I have discovered further inland at Kilballyowen in much denser vegetation. The Trailing Tormentil (*Potentilla anglica*) does not take root along its creeping stem. Tormentil, is delicate, yet hardy, surviving the hostilities of exposed moors without damage to its fresh beauty. It has a very long flowering season from April to September and its root has been used as a red dye for leather. It is also known to be used in herbal medicine as a cure for several ailments.

OPEN PEATY MOORS AND OTHER LOW VEGETATION AREAS

The tiny Bog Pimpernel

Bog Pimpernel (*Anagallis tenella*) mingled on the Ross Moors with White Clover, Plantains and Heathers

Almost microscopic in stature, Bog Pimpernel inhabits the moors off the Eastern track from the Bridges of Ross car park and is also prevalent on near bare peaty patches on the open plains behind Loophead Lighthouse. I first discovered this plant with James in 2010, and it had not registered any youthful recalling of previous sightings. This creeping carpet forming plant is trodden on by the unsuspecting visitor, not realizing its presence underfoot. One therefore needs to tread carefully on these Moors to ensure Bog

Pimpernel continues to mesmerize us with its tiny yet sublime existence. Bog Pimpernel is composed of cup-like flowers which are five lobed and white but heavily veined with crimson therefore the flower appears pink in colour. The flowers are solitary at the end of stalks and have a mass of white stamens at the centre. A ground covering trailing herb that roots at the nodes, and member of the Primrose family, its even tinier leaves are mostly rounded approx 5mm in diameter and appear in opposite pairs. Bog Pimpernel likes damp peaty ground, like that found at Ross and in patches at Loophead, and can be found scattered and locally frequent on the Western and Southern coasts of both Ireland and Britain. One lives in awe at the raw delicacy and the ambitious intentions of Bog Pimpernel to reside in our midst, hidden in low vegetation, yet hugely exposed to every considerable threat from nature itself and the human trampling upon it.

OPEN PEATY MOORS AND OTHER LOW VEGETATION AREAS

Red Fescue *(Festuca rubra)*

Red Fescue is the dominant grass on both the Ross and Loophead Moors. It forms dense springy tufts which softens the underfoot conditions, and forms peaks and troughs on the moor which are shaped by wind orientation. The grass is very wiry, shiny, needle-like, and a rich green colour. Because of these features the sward is unpalatable to livestock. Because it is allowed to prosper un-manicured and mostly un-grazed by animals, its long wiry leaves which can grow to 30cm flop over. With its creeping root system, it has the ability to bind soil and is therefore a useful deterrent against coastal erosion. Red Fescue forms a dense mat of verdant vegetation at Ross and Loophead.

Sea Campion *(Silene uniflora)* nestled in Red Fescue Grass *(Festuca rubra)* at Ross

Perhaps for me defining the ultimate wild flower, the elusive nature of the Sea Campion crops up here and there mostly nestled in the Red Fescue grass, with only its delicate and intricate flower head showing. What is elusive and so random about this plant is the fact that each year I return to look for this plant, it has departed its previous settling and moved onto a different location. In fact in 2010, it barely had any presence on the moors at Ross. I have yet to find Sea Campion on the moors at Loophead. Pulling away the grass, to look at the entire above ground structure of this chirpy plant, one finds a sturdy, yet thin upright stem with paired oblong leaves on it. Just below the white flower is a very distinctive calyx ribbed tube which has a fleshy colouring. Its flower head is relatively large - up to 2.5cm in diameter and is pure white in colour with five heart-shaped petals and approx ten stamens. A member of the Campion family, which also includes Chickweeds, Stitchworts, and the Ragged Robin, Sea Campion forms an unkept like appearance mingled with the Red Fescue, instilling in me a great inner sense of its marvelous free spirit. James and I have also spotted from time to time, Sea Campion on the loose shingle outside Rhynvella Beach.

Bird's-foot Trefoil

One of the key properties of Bird's-foot Trefoil is its ability to shine like the sun, albeit facing the sky and not from the sky! This is one of my 'sunshine' plants, brilliant yellow flowering plants that instil a sense of sunshine even on damp drizzly days. I have known this plant for as long as I can remember, associating it in particular with the Eastern track from the Bridges of Ross car park, just there, mingling the Heathers, Silverweed, Plantains and White Clover and whatever else you might find. However, whilst enjoying the dry peaty soils of this area, Bird's-foot Trefoil, is not too fussy about its habitat, and I have found it on grassy margins, on stony beaches and places far away from the coast. Nothing could brighten your day of nature trekking more than meeting this 'sunshine' plant time and again.

Bird's-foot Trefoil *(Lotus corniculatus)* dazzling from the ground up.

Also abundant on the moors at Loophead, especially the South Eastern moor, down closer to the ocean, Bird's-foot Trefoil, is a member of the rather large Pea family, and has been labeled with many common names like 'Birds Claws', 'Rabbits Ears', Bacon and Eggs' and 'Tom Thumb'. Its true name arose, because after flowering, the seed pods are arranged in a birds foot pattern. This plant is a sprawling perennial, with trailing short stems 10-40cm long. With a long flowering period, from approx mid-April to September, its early clustered flowers have tinges of red, orange and crimson. Its leaflets are round to slightly oval and small, on a stem that is woody at the base. The flowers of Meadow Vetchling can look very similar to Bird's-foot Trefoil, but its leaves are long thin lanceolate shaped leaves. Both plants are very common in the Peninsula. Bees and especially butterflies visit each flower several times to collect the flower's abundant nectar. The plant is highly toxic to humans.

OPEN PEATY MOORS AND OTHER LOW VEGETATION AREAS

Wild Thyme

Nothing infuses the moors with more rich and intense colour than a tightly knitted clump of Wild Thyme. Enjoying thin soils and peaty hummocks, it often forms itself around outcropped rocks, low vegetation ditches near the moors and sporadically on the moor. On studying this herb closely, when in bloom, one finds a tightly knitted cluster of cerise-purple-lavender coloured four petalled, flat-faced flower heads protecting its tiny oval hairy leaves and short stems. This is a mat forming creeping plant, with stems to 10cm long growing to 2cm tall. It is a member of the Dead Nettle Family, a family shared with Mints, Wild Majoram, Self Heal, Dead Nettles and Woundworts, few of which show up anywhere in the Loophead Peninsula.

James and I have found Wild Thyme at various locations, including the Eastern and Western moors at Ross, at the top of the bothárin leading to the

A crop of Wild Thyme *(Thymus polytrichus)* on the Western Moor s at Ross

car park, at Loophead - on the South East facing moor East and South of the Lighthouse. We have also discovered it on the roadside on Fodera Hill in waste shingle ground. Wild Thyme is a delicately scented plant, and if you give it a rub over with your hand, you will experience this smell which is not as strong as the garden Thyme most used as a culinary herb. The herb is native to most of Europe, growing at high altitudes. Wild Thyme has medicinal uses, when distilled, and its dried leaves are used in a herbal tea which is quite popular. It is also an important source of nectar for bees. In folklore, Wild Thyme was revered as a plant which marked the favourite visitation sites for faeries. Land decorated with the herb was said to be blessed as sacred by faeries and large gatherings were held at such locations, where attendees smeared themselves in Thyme Oil!

Where have those good old days gone?

Being on the moor tops spotting the tiny flora, one is never more than a stones throw from an ocean view, whilst all the time being accompanied by the fresh ocean smells and crispy breezes that sometimes may feel more stormy. At the end of the Eastern track at the Bridges of Ross, one meets with this mesmerizing scene of raw, rich beauty. The straight lines of the ancient layered and ocean sculpted rock, juxtaposing with lichen coated rounded clumsy outcropped rocks at the end of the moor. Then the smooth quarried lunar like surface of the inner rock field side by side with the whisked each way Red Fescue grass and dimpled slate blue moving ocean. Sometimes I stand here feeling that I am the one moving.

OPEN PEATY MOORS AND OTHER LOW VEGETATION AREAS

This little 'Clover' like flower, which is a member of the Pea family, and therefore related to both Vetches and Clover, has very silky leaves and stems. The leaves have a slightly Vetch-like appearance - with several paired linear-oblong leaflets attached to the stem. At the end of each stem is a dense rounded clover-like flower head, with petals ranging in colour from soft yellow to deep yellow, orange, rust and crimson, shooting from a woolly white calyx tube.

Flowering from May to September, Kidney Vetch can be found sporadically in small spreading, trailing clumps on the moors at the Bridges of Ross and Loophead, and less frequently on grass margins near the coast. Mostly a coastal plant, it does however like limestone soils, and can be found in abundance at such sites including the Burren and the Aran Islands. Kidney Vetch has rich medicinal qualities, and it has been used to relieve spasms, detoxify, reduce swelling, and promote wound healing. The red tips of Kidney Vetch were thought to resemble flecks of blood and hence its usage as a remedy to stop bleeding and heal skin wounds. Kidney Vetch can be used both internally - as a tea using the flowering tops - and externally on the skin. Indeed one wonders about the free availability of many such herbal remedy plants in our midst, our general removal from the knowledge of their healing powers which remain almost hidden secrets within the plants themselves.

Kidney Vetch (*Anthyllis vulneraria*) on the Ross Moors

Little did James and I know that as we visited this rather large and singular plant living on the edge of the car park of the Bridges of Ross over the past few years, and unable to identify it, that this herb was of such fascinating ancient medicinal repute. Featuring in Greek and Roman literature and poetry, Pliny the Elder, who was a Roman author, naturalist and natural philosopher declared of the plant 'Let no day pass without eating some of the roots of Inula, considered to help digestion and cause mirth'! He also declared that 'the root being chewed fasting, doth fasten the teeth'!

This plant which sits uncomfortably on the grassy cliff edge, being whisked every which way by the constant winds, burning the edges of its gigantic leaves in the process, has through the centuries been formally cultivated in private herb-gardens, as a culinary and medicinal plant. Elecampane is the greatest natural source of inulin, a polysaccharide, used increasingly in processed foods, that can be used to replace sugar, fat and flour. Inulin also has health benefits, increasing calcium absorption and promoting growth of intestinal bacteria. In more recent times, research at Cork Institute of Technology, has shown that extracts from the herb kill MRSA, and a broad range of other bacteria. The parts used in herbal medicine are the flowers- harvested in Summer at their peak of blooming and the root - harvested in the Autumn.

A gigantic member of the Daisy Family (Asteraceae), this particular plant is dwarfed by its hostile environment, growing only 30-40cm tall, when the normal range is 60-150cm tall. It has strong stout stems, large oval clasping and deeply veined leaves, with very large golden yellow dandelion-like flower heads (6-8cm) with many rays which are notched at the edges. It was summer 2010, when we finally identified this plant, which, according to the BSBI distribution maps, is by no means common in the British Isles nowadays.

Elecampane *(Inula helenium)* at the Bridges of Ross - an ancient Herbal

OPEN PEATY MOORS AND OTHER LOW VEGETATION AREAS

Devil's-bit Scabious is a late flowering blue plant on the moors at Ross, flowering from mid-August onward. Almost inconspicious, by its dwarfed size, on meeting Devil's-bit Scabious in the Burren, for instance, one finds a tall upright plant with a tall strong stem slightly branched that you cannot miss. Devil's-bit Scabious at Ross, has dug itself low onto the open unsheltered windy moors, and splays itself wider to compensate. Its leaves are oval and downy and clasping the stem. The rounded flower heads are composite and tightly tucked in a dense hard berry-like form before flowering. Liking damp peaty soils, it has a tap root which is short and looks like something has bitten the end off - The Devil -. When James and I first encountered Devil's-bit Scabious at Ross in 2008, it was tall and growing on a mud heap abandoned at the car park, and later removed, so it was 2011before we encountered this dwarfed version of the plant which had spread itself over a wide area near the Poll Gorm. A member of the Teasel Family, we have not recorded Devil's-bit Scabious on the moors at Loophead.

Although some plants, that we have met on our travels are not as showy in their output of colour, they are nonetheless attractive and delicate by way of their natural formation and detail and muted colour. This is the case with Sea Plantain, found sporadically on the moors at Ross and Loophead, with its dense basal rosette of long narrow leaves and dull textured long stalked flowers, which have soft yellow-green stamens. This formation contrasts well with the tight clumps of Wild Thyme, English Stonecrop, and Sea Thrift, adding height to low growth sheltered areas. A member of the Plantain family, all of whom like coastal habitats, Sea Plantain, can be harvested, cooked and eaten. If grazing or foraging for wild food on the moors, is your thing, Sea Plantain, is one of those wild plants that serves up a delicious meal cooked as a risotto, for example, or just eaten raw. It is perhaps time that we all re-learn the lost art of foraging, healing and celebrating with wild plants, and return our senses to the natural world.

Above - Devil's-bit Scabious (*Succisa pratensis*)- Below - Sea Plantain*(Plantago maritima)*

Eyebright *(Euphrasia agg.)*

These tiny pretty plants are found mostly on nearly bare moor top at the Bridges of Ross, where there is abundance of them especially on the eastern track from the car park. No doubt a tough little plant to survive in this environment, it is however, semi-parasitic, feeding off the roots of nearby grasses and thereby keeping their growth in check. Flowers May -September.

The Eyebright has oval sharply toothed leaves, and pretty white flowers which are two lipped and have purple veins, and a deep yellow centre. Eyebright is a member of the Figwort Family, and there are as many as forty varieties of Eyebright, and I have seen much taller species elsewhere in the County. Eyebright has a long interesting history, and it has been most commonly linked with the treatment of blindness, and an ancient paper on the virtues of Eyebright entitled *'Vini Euphrasiati tantopere celebrati'* by Arnoldus Villanovanus stated that *'it hath restored sight to them that have been blind a long time'*. Hildamus believed that it would restore the sight to many people who were seventy or eighty years old. It was also thought by Culpepper to strengthen the weak brain or memory. Eyebright tea was, and still is used and available from health food stores. Most modern herbalists highly recommend Eyebright, and ongoing research on its use and value is being carried out.

You will be drawn to the majestic remaining natural bridge at the Bridges of Ross whilst on these moors heading towards Ross Point.

Cat's-ear (*Hypochaeris radicata*) on the cliff edge at Ross

As natural explorers, with no scientific background, it is really important to look at wild flowers very closely, recording leaf shape, whether it is smooth or hairy, smooth on one side and hairy on the other, whether the leaves form a basal rosette, or are paired along the stem, or are stem clasping or have petioles. Likewise, the stem needs to be studied, determining its length, thickness and branches(if any), and other details. Finally the flowers are examined, clustered or singular, dense or loose forming, spiked, florets, umbels, colour, stamens, and so forth. This is necessary, to enable accurate identification of plants for your records. This systematic type of inspection of the above Dandelion-like flower, led us in the end to its identification. On close examination, we found that the stem was not hollow in the centre like the Dandelion. We found that the stem was straggly and branched - unlike that of the Dandelion which is both tuberous and mostly erect. We found that the leaves were densely hairy, like that of a cat's ear to the touch (hence the name of this plant), and were not as lobed in shape as those of the Dandelion. Sporadically growing on the edge of the moors at Ross and on nearby ditches, not recorded at Loophead.

OPEN PEATY MOORS AND OTHER LOW VEGETATION AREAS

Navelwort, a highly distinctive, easily recognized fleshy plant, which is a member of the succulent Stonecrop Family can be occasionally found growing out of the bare stone ditch on the shady Western side of the botharín leading to the Bridges of Ross car park. The tubular flowers are soft creamy green in colour growing out of a long central stalk. The leaves at the base of the flowering stem are fleshy and round and are pulled in a 'navel like' depression at the centre. These leaves bear a striking resemblance to those of Marsh Pennywort, which also frequent the moors at Loophead and Ross. A creeping and rooting perennial, its distinctive leaves occupy low growth and almost bare vegetation areas on the moors. It is however, classed as a member of the Carrot Family. A perennial herb, Navelwort is also known as Wall Pennywort. Like many of the other wild plants, mentioned in this book, Navelwort has since ancient times been researched and noted for its medicinal properties. From healing pimples, to cooling high temperatures and burning pains, Navelwort can be distilled, or juice extracted, formed into ointment or simply used depressed against skin wounds to stop bleeding.

Marsh Pennywort *(Hydrocotyle vulgaris)* on the moors at Ross.

Navelwort *(Umbilicus rupestris)* on a stone wall at Ross

46

Of all members of the vetches and vetchling species that are found in the Western Loophead Region, the Common Vetch has the rarest showing here. Other vetches and vetchlings present include the Meadow Vetchling, Kidney Vetch, Tufted Vetch and Bush Vetch. This significant Vetch had climbed to a height of approx two meters just to the Western end of the Bridges of Ross car park and being supported all the way by tall grassy and Bramble vegetation. This upward growth takes place because the tendrils of the Common Vetch latch themselves onto taller growing plants. This particular plant is a lusciously green coloured, paired leaved, bright pink blossoming one, with clambering tendrils at the end of each leaf stalk. The stems are ribbed and the leaves are slightly hairy. The pealike flowers are mostly in clusters of three. The flower corolla is a stronger pink. Although not a moorland plant, I have included Common Vetch in this section because it is just at the entrance to the Western moors.

The Common Vetch is an excellent fodder for horses and cattle, better than the Red Clover, for instance, and it is grown as part of a grazing crop feed, because fattening cattle feed faster on Vetch than most grasses or edible plants. The leaf constituent is grass-like. If there are no tall crops surrounding the Common Vetch it becomes a low-growing sprawling plant.

This is a spectacular plant to observe, such a network of branching stems latching onto surrounding growth, displaying a magnificent and delicate leaf formation of 4 -8 pairs of leaflets per leaf stalk. Yet it is the bright pink flower that calls one to its attention. It becomes complicated to identify from a congregation of 140 worldwide species of the vetches.

It has been shown that this plant too, was consumed by humans in times past. Through testing remains found at early Neolithic sites in the Middle East and Eastern Europe, and Bronze Age sites, from Western Asia, Common Vetch was found to be part of the human diet in each instance.

Common Vetch (*Vicia sativa*) at Ross

OPEN PEATY MOORS AND OTHER LOW VEGETATION AREAS

Tufted Vetch (*Vicia cracca*) common across several habitats

Spreading its jewel-coloured violet blue/lavender flowers across several habitats, it is always an uplifting surprise to encounter Tufted Vetch. With a long flowering period, from May to September, and cropping up everywhere from the cliff tops at Ross, to the wall side growth at Loophead Lighthouse, to the waysides and farmlands, this delicately formed, yet robustly capable plant, captivates the imagination with its entangled growth patterns. Tufted Vetch is normally bushy and sprawling, clasping its tendrils onto stronger leaves and other growth allowing itself a greater view of a higher environment.

Tufted Vetch has weak stems, and therefore needs support from those plants around it, sometimes clasping onto itself, if no other support is available. A popular member of the Pea Family, it is more easily recognisable than some of its comrades with a single sided long raceme display of 10-40 lavender/blue violet flowers. Its paired oblong leaflets are similar to, but smaller than those of the Common Vetch, forming eight to thirteen pairs along each leaf stalk. The Tufted Vetch is one of the few wild flowers that can still be seen in grazing farmlands, where it is known to produce Nitrogen-rich fodder for cattle.

OPEN PEATY MOORS AND OTHER LOW VEGETATION AREAS

Lesser Spearwort, a member of the Buttercup Family, frequents damp soggy parts of the moors at both Ross and Loophead. This plant which has spread itself in prostrate form close to the surface of the moor, can also be found in an erect form but not on these exposed moors. The plant, which is poisonous to cattle and sheep, differs from other members of the Buttercup family in having lanceolate shaped leaves, compared with the divided lobed leaves of the Buttercup. It has five rounded lemon-yellow petals which are more flat than cup-like and an attractive centre dome of yellow stamens. Flowering from April to September, one has to really look closely on the nearly bare surface turf to find this flower.

By contrast with the Lesser Spearwort, Silverweed is one of the most frequent plants that you will encounter anywhere, from the moor tops to the road margins and beach shingle and far away from the coastline. This attractive plant, and member of the Rose family, has distinctive pinnate, silky, silvery leaves, and creeps along by rooting at the nodes of its russet coloured stem. An immensely important plant in herbal medicine, every part of the plant has been used in tea or in a cooked form to treat a whole host of ailments and to use as a tonic.

Silverweed *(Potentilla anserina)*

Lesser Spearwort *(Ranunculus flammula)*

The pinnate shaped leaves of Silverweed are spectacular and consist of several paired toothed oblong leaflets arranged around the leaf stem with a terminal leaflet. These leaves are often russet tinged in full sun exposure.

The distant sloping, jagged and horizontal lines of Kerry separated by the Mouth of the Shannon River as it joins the Atlantic Ocean at Loophead while James walks the moors accompanied by a sea of Irish Marsh Orchids.

OPEN PEATY MOORS AND OTHER LOW VEGETATION AREAS

THE LOOPHEAD MOORS

Although barely separated by a couple of kilometers, difference takes its foothold, as the far greater sized moors at Loophead present a floral footprint that varies from those at Ross. The moors at Loophead slope steeply to the South of the Lighthouse towards the Hanging Gardens, while just behind the Lighthouse the decline is a lot less pronounced. There is great vegetative variation within these moors: to the East, on both sides of the road approaching the Lighthouse, we have the rare and delicate topography of a wind sculpted 'tufted moor' area, which spends most of the year waterlogged, and barely supports, the Heathers, Wild Thyme and sparsely populated Tormentil. Just West of the Lighthouse wall and roaming South West towards the Ocean, one finds tall vegetation including various Summer grasses, Red Fescue, Yarrow, Sneezewort, Oraches, Plantains and Burdock. As one proceeds toward the most Westerly point and away from the beaten track, towards the Ocean, one finds salt-marshy like soggy conditions, and the only habitat of the lovely Sea Aster, that we have found in the Peninsula. Also here one finds the stiff, upright Sea Arrowgrass and if you are lucky a wonderful sea of White Clover. Where vegetation is low to bare, you will be in the company of Bird's-foot Trefoil, Kidney Vetch, Lesser Spearwort, Wild Thyme, Sea Pinks, Common Mouse-ear, Marsh Pennywort, Bog Pimpernel, Tormentil and the short seasoned Irish Marsh Orchid which vigorously inhabits these moors. Further East on the approach to Loophead Lighthouse, you may encounter Japanese Rose, Fleabane, Bog Cotton and Sheep's-bit. The moors will always be sprinkled with Bell Heather and Ling. Whilst on the moors at Loophead, don't forget to keep an eye on the ocean, where a pod of bottle nose Dolphins may be on a northbound trip, or further out on the ocean a Humpback Whale may be performing acrobatics, or to the sky where the sleek movements of the Fulmars, will

Irish Marsh Orchid (*Dactylorhiza occidentalis*) is abundant at Loophead

entrance your undivided attention for several minutes. In early-mid June, the visitor can experience a dense population of Irish Marsh Orchids, intermingling the low growing grasses especially North West and West of the Lighthouse. A visual treat, these Orchids do not occur on the Ross Moors. The Irish Marsh Orchid enjoys damp, marshy and peaty soils, and presents itself as a dense purple fatted flower spike with a robust fleshy stem and black/brown spotted fleshy long oblong leaves. Close examination of this magical flower, will reveal exquisite pattern detail on each flower lobe which is one of its distinguishing features.

'The colourful crop of Sea Pinks (Thrift) (*Armeria maritima*)- colouring the Moors at Loophead - May 2010

OPEN PEATY MOORS AND OTHER LOW VEGETATION AREAS

Thrift - Sea Pinks (*Armeria maritima*) on the Loophead Moors

Not found more than two hundred metres away from the sea, and typically within a fifty metre range, Thrift, also commonly known as Sea Pink, is the ultimate coastal plant. Forming tufted cushions, with woody roots, and a basal mat of shiny needle-like leaves out of which grows a long silk stalk that supports a rounded mid-pink clustered flower head of five petaled pink flowers with soft yellow stamens. Thrift can form luxuriously large hummocks on the moors at Loophead, on the ditches close to the ocean front along the coastline roads in the Peninsula, on the Ross moors, down the vertical cliff faces, in rock crevices and cliff edges, providing a refreshing floral display from late April to mid June, being at their best during the month of May. There are always late bloomers and an odd faded pink bunch of Thrift can be found right through the Summer months. Indeed James and I have found them blooming in November. This plant is very tolerant of salt and strong winds and will venture down close to the tide-line. There is nothing more intoxicating than spending a blue sky day on the moors in the midst of Thrift, one feels like rolling among them and roaring felicities to the Heavens!

Sea Aster (*Aster tripolium*) on the moors at Loophead

Unless one wanders off the beaten track on the expansive moors at Loophead, one will not discover the only settling of Sea Aster that we have found in the Loophead Peninsula. Loving salt marsh, and cliff top conditions, the Sea Aster at Loophead can be found North West of the Lighthouse in a wet marshy area which is also home to the Sea Arrowgrass and a large sea of White Clover, which frequent this particular patch of the moors. The Sea Aster puts on a gorgeous display, flowering from mid July to September, this soft lilac and mustard daisy like flower head has a profuse settling in this particular marshy patch. It is a strong, oblong, fleshy leaved plant growing to approx 20cm high, the flower heads are loosely clustered. Apparently, the leaves of Sea Aster, are a most tasty ingredient of 'gourmet foraging' dishes, being quickly fried, in butter and flavourings, and served with fish and other dishes or on their own. It was September 2008, when James and I first discovered the habitation of Sea Aster at Loophead, and it was just about going off Season at the time. We have connected with this very special plant each year since. A member of the Daisy (Asteraceae) Family, and very similar in appearance to the garden Michelmas Daisy.

There is a sense of intrigue about this tall, slender, fleshy and stiffly upright plant occupying a small wet low lying and low vegetation area on the Loophead moors. Sea Arrowgrass has a basal rosette of linear leaves, and its green-purple flowers are three petalled. This potentially poisonous plant which mostly frequents salt marshes, has a very dense spike of flowers which present from May to September. A perennial and member of the Juncaginaceae family, it does not grow inland. Looking similar in appearance to Sea Plantain, the green leaves of the plant can contain a toxic cyanogenic glycoside, especially during drought periods. The ashes of this plant are rich in potassium and can be used for making soap. The habitation of Sea Arrowgrass on the Loophead moors can be found West of the Lighthouse, and deep in the moors, in a wet area close to the Sea Aster habitation. It has not been found on the Ross moors. Looking at Sea Arrowgrass on the moors reminds me of a druid-like land occupation, where the self important Arrowgrass, stands tall and important and almost curvaceously seated on its throne. The soggy conditions around it prevent too much human invasion.

Sea Arrowgrass (*Triglochin maritimum*) at Loophead

Frosted Orache (*Atriplex laciniata*)

White Clover (*Trifolium repens*)

Our first encounter with Frosted Orache, a member of the Goosefoot Family, was on the moors at Loophead, in 2008, hidden in the Red Fescue but outstanding because of its unusual colouring and formation. This is actually an unusual habitat for this plant, which prefers shingle beaches, like at Rhynvella, and beach tops, where one can visualise the entire plant in its more natural form. At Loophead the more sheltered Orache, displays its 'sugar frosted' leaves which are silvery grey, wavy edged and diamond shaped. It has a sprawling growth habit rather than upright. It flowers from July to September displaying a spike of tiny flowers. Its stems are normally red tinged, but this Orache which is more hidden from an exposed sun has a pale green/grey stem. It is a fleshy plant, which is extremely tolerant of salt content in the ground and retains salt in its leaves. As a coastal plant, it is less common on our West coasts. James and I have also found Frosted Orache on the loose shingle outside Rhynvella Beach (as pictured above) where it thrives side by side with Spear-Leaved Orache.

By no means confined to the moors at Loophead or indeed coastal areas, I nonetheless wished to include White Clover in this chapter and at this location, because of the profuse flowering patch of White Clover that James and I discovered on the Loophead moors in the same area as the Sea Aster and not seen anywhere else in such a glorious display and really begging us to roll in its soft knitted carpet. This trifoliate plant, with a distinctive crescent marking on its leaves is a creeping and rooting perennial. White Clover which survives well in very poor mineral soil, has a densely clustered spherical head of white flowers, tinged with russet, scented and at the end of long weak hairless stalks. A member of the Pea family, which includes Vetches, Clovers and Gorse, and all common in the area. White Clover also frequents low vegetation verges, and lawns, preferring to be surrounded by much lower vegetation than the Red Clover. The White Clover has a rich folklore, and was held in high esteem by the early Celts as a charm against evil spirits and in bringing good luck. This pagan tradition was continued by early Christian leaders until it became the symbol of the Holy Trinity for Irish Christianity.

Heather(Ling) is tough, wiry and sprawling over large patches of the peaty moor at Loophead and also Ross. This is the natural habitat of this plant, with its much tangled reddish stems, and loose spikes of soft lavender/purple flowers which appear from August to September. Heather frequents peatland, which is usually permanently wet. Proximity to the Atlantic Ocean causes this 'Oceanicity' of damp air flows from the sea to land at Loophead. These moors are fragile and would have formed over centuries of new layers of vegetation over dead layers of vegetation, or new layers forming over living vegetative layers. Part of the tufted moor East of the Lighthouse was harvested as a turf bog during the earlier part of the last century. In fact the uses to which Heather has been put are many, it was once an important part of the economy in areas where it flourished, being used for the making of sweeping brushes, homemade tea, a flavouring for ale, an orange dye for baskets, a thatching material and stuffing mattresses making comfortable fragrant beds. Our predecessors worked ingeniously to employ local and abundantly available plants into their limited resource bank.

Being on the tufted moors at Loophead, one experiences a rare topography together with a sense of space and solitude. The tufted moors are generally East of the Lighthouse on both sides of the approach road. The soil is very thin and gravelly and the tufted mounds of Heathers normally provide the main vegetation. Another member of the Heath family sharing this space with the Ling is Bell Heather, a shorter plant with dense tiny dark green foliage of needle-like leaves bunching around its reddened stems. Bell Heather stands out more because of its larger and bell-shaped cerise coloured flowers that bloom from April to September. Heather has a long life span and can survive up to forty years.

A much rarer Heath that I have located on these Moors is a White Cross Leaved Heath with four leaved whorls along its stem. This Heath is also present in a pink hue.

Above: Heather (Ling) *(Calluna vulgaris)* Below: Bell Heather *(Erica cinerea)*

Sneezewort (*Achillea ptarmica*)

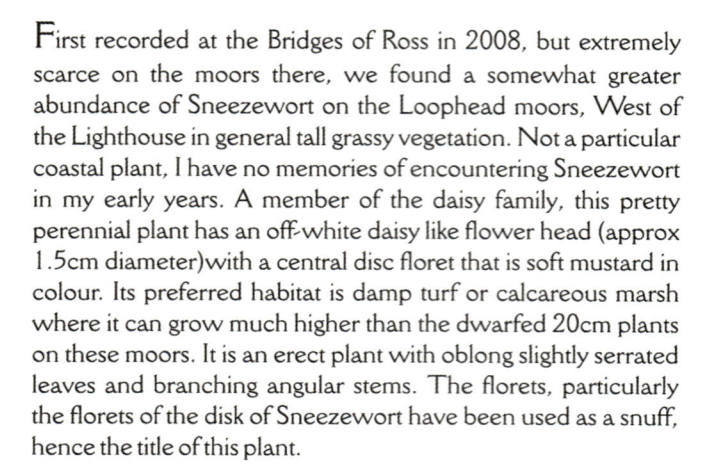

Yarrow (*Achillea millefolium*)

First recorded at the Bridges of Ross in 2008, but extremely scarce on the moors there, we found a somewhat greater abundance of Sneezewort on the Loophead moors, West of the Lighthouse in general tall grassy vegetation. Not a particular coastal plant, I have no memories of encountering Sneezewort in my early years. A member of the daisy family, this pretty perennial plant has an off-white daisy like flower head (approx 1.5cm diameter) with a central disc floret that is soft mustard in colour. Its preferred habitat is damp turf or calcareous marsh where it can grow much higher than the dwarfed 20cm plants on these moors. It is an erect plant with oblong slightly serrated leaves and branching angular stems. The florets, particularly the florets of the disk of Sneezewort have been used as a snuff, hence the title of this plant.

Sneezewort and Yarrow are very closely related, but Yarrow has a dense umbel-like clustered floret and bushy finely divided leaves. James and I have found a far greater bounty of Yarrow, on the moors at Loophead, rarely on the Ross moors and on various hedgerows and ditches throughout the Peninsula. Its flowering colour varies from soft pink to soft creamy white with tiny daisy-like flower heads. A very pretty plant, and one of our favourites, it is aromatic, and widely regarded in herbal medicine. The leaves can be dried and used as a herbal Yarrow tea, to help cure Winter's colds and flu. In the middle ages, both the Greeks and Romans used it to stop bleeding. It was also used in beer making before the widespread use of hops. In Celtic Folklore, it was thought that Yarrow had the ability to banish negative forces!

OPEN PEATY MOORS AND OTHER LOW VEGETATION AREAS

There are some notable plants, worth mentioning, that have only a small presence at Loophead. For instance, Bog Cotton, which is in fact a member of the Sedge family, raises its head above the low vegetation moor and provides a joyous dance in the Summer breeze. Only found East, on the moors approaching the lighthouse, It has a narrow, erect, hairless and leafless stem of a deep crimson colour, topped by a white cottony seeded flower head.

Lesser Burdock is also a rare showing flower at Loophead, where I have discovered this particular plant sheltered against the South facing wall leading down to the South Western Moors. Nestled among Nettles and other flora, Lesser Burdock grows to approx half a metre, has large oval-cordate soft non-prickly and slightly wrinkled looking leaves, that are a bright rich green shade. The stem is strong, oval and tinged ruby wine in colour. The flower heads are quite spiny and deep pink and have a 'Thistle-like' appearance. The brown bracts at the base of the flower head form spiky burrs that easily attach themselves onto clothing and animal fur, and have to be plucked off or dispersed elsewhere by the animals carrying them. This tall robust plant is a member of the Daisy family.

Bog Cotton *(Eriophorum angustifolium)*

Lesser Burdock *(Arctium minus)*

'A calm day at the species-rich habitat of Ross Beach looking towards Fodera Hill

Chapter 4 - Rocky, Stony and Sandy Beaches

ROSS BEACH

Ross Beach provides a stony & rocky edged inlet bordering the roadway between the townland of Ross and Moneen leading to Kilbaha. Having grown up less than one hundred metres away from this beach, and passing it at least twice daily on my way to and from school, church and shop, I feel I possess an understanding of its moods and movements, its cache of seashore treasure, its temper and tantrums, its power and serenity. One feels its continuous presence, and one learns to respect its immense power and influence.

My memories of school days are full of the fears of passing by this ocean side at morning and evening while on my school journey. At the head of Ross Beach, there were but a mound of loose beach stones, no protective cliffs, and the land all around it is low lying. During ocean storms and high tides, the stormy seas, did not obey this makeshift, self created mound, and at least once each year during my young school days, the ocean drove wildly and blindly beyond the top of the beach driving the loose stones, seaweeds and ocean debris across the road and well onto the fields at the other side. This meant that the road had to be closed. One worry I had was that this would happen during school hours, and then I would not be able to return home, Other times, I worried that this would happen while we were coming home from school, and we would be swept away with the furious and powerful tide. Neither happened. But each Winter, we spent days home from school because the beach road had to be closed. Other times we were lashed with frothy foam, driven by the wind in off the ocean. At nighttime, the deep and scary dragging of the ocean bed as the ocean retreated to re-mount its inward invasion, coupled with the final lash back, meant many sleepless hours. The fear that the next wave was to envelop our house, as they sounded so powerful and near, was unfounded.

In the past ten to fifteen years, the beach boundary was re-enforced with gabions, (wire-netted stone ditches), that help enormously to protect the roadside during ocean storms. There is still an overspill though during very rough high Spring seas.

Experiencing a serene, pleasant, peaceful ocean, has also been of immense influence. In childhood days, these special times were spent with my mum, whereby we would spend an entire pleasant Sunday afternoon, studying and walking the coastline from the Bridges of Ross to Ross Beach, taking in the birds, the flowers, rocks, pretty white stones, and sea shells. The atmospheric combination of soft silken breezes, ocean smells, bright skies, gently rippling and glistening waters, and ong necked birds perched on faraway rocks whilst we rummaged for perfect sea shells or discussed life's little details was blissfully removed from the hustle and bustle of the farmyard.

Today, James and I research Ross Beach from a slightly more scientific perspective. Our eyes are drawn to the detail of the Orange Leafy Lichen, the Black Tar Lichen, Sea Ivory, the Tangle Kelp, Channel Wrack, the jagged shale rock formation, the tide line, the Seals in the bay, the salt marsh, and the rich bio-diversity bounding the tide line. Ross Beach is simply a very species-rich and pure habitat. Although perhaps not as colourful as other locations, Ross Beach has its own combination of wild flora and sea vegetables, not found elsewhere in the Peninsula. On the outer roadside, on the loose shingle, there is the main home of Sea Mayweed, Perennial Sow Thistle, Curled Dock, Sea Bindweed and Broad Leaf Plantain, inside above the tide-line, lives Bittersweet, Spear-leaved Orache, Sea Milkwort, Silverweed, Sea Beet, Rock Samphire and others.

On a Stony Beach

On a warm gentle July day
I wander my way to Ross Bay
with four young cousins and a happy dog
seeking pleasure on the stony plot.

The cousins four and the giddy dog
reach down to the waters edge
where stones they'll throw, while the waters flow
long into the evening fog.

I will wander further on
to the serrated outcropped ponded rock
and there I'll gaze at nature's grace
on this Godly day in my native place.

Sitting there on the rocky shore
where ripples barely splash and trickle
and a deeper sound from the distance pounds
and my mind floats onto the surface fickle.

To lose oneself to the ocean ripples
to drench ones thoughts in their soothing spell
is to float like a shimmer on a transparent memoir
long into the evening fog.

(2010)

Rock Samphire

Rock Samphire *(Crithmum maritimum)* at Ross Beach

Unlike Samuel Lewis, writing in the 'Topographical Dictionary of Ireland' in 1837, whereby when describing the parish of Kilballyowen, he singled out that Samphire of a superior quality was to be found on the cliffs at Clohansevan, (approx 2km North East of Ross Beach), I have not found Rock Samphire in any great quantity in the region. Rock Samphire often occupies precarious cliff sides facing the ocean, and quite inaccessible. There is a colonization of it in such conditions at the Bridges, on the Eastern side of the Bridge itself. However, this plant was photographed at Ross Beach, growing through the loose stones on the Eastern side of the beach in full sun. Rock Samphire is a valuable edible vegetable, and in times past, lives have been lost harvesting this plant for city markets. It has been referred to several times in historical writings including Shakespeare who referred to it growing on the White Cliffs of Dover. In 1597 Gerard wrote ' The leaves kept in pickle and eaten in salads with oile and vinegar is a pleasant sauce for meat, wholesome for the stoppings of the liver, milt and kidnys. Samphire leaves look like succulents and are at their best and freshest in Spring, until early Summer before the plant flowers' Rock Samphire, is a fleshy, bushy plant that tolerates heavily salted soils and salt laden winds. It has an umbel like flower head of tiny creamy green flowers and is a member of the Carrot family. Nowadays, as a relatively rare sea vegetable related to parsley and fennel, it is sought in 'Gourmet Foraging' and is normally simmered for seven to eight minutes and then fried in butter with seasoning and it is said that it accompanies white fish dishes particularly well.

63

ROCKY, STONY AND SANDY BEACHES

Ross Beach - Limpets, Barnacles, Serrated Wrack, Beadlet Anemones, Dilisk and Encrusting Seaweeds providing a species-rich habitat.

Beadlet Anemones and seaweed-encrusted beach stones

Sea Mayweed (*Tripleurospermum maritimum*)

Sea Mayweed, has by far its largest colonization at Ross Beach. Such a pretty, flamboyant and noticeable plant, I have encountered Sea Mayweed for as long as I can remember on the loose shingle roadside at Ross Beach, in great quantity, its feathery, finely divided and shiny leaves, flippantly waving in the breeze, whilst its large (4-6cm) flower heads, encourage an upbeat, high Summer lifting of Spirits! In fact, with its white petals folded back, it reminds me of a friendly dog greeting its master! With dense mustard disc florets, bounded by white ray florets, this showy plant is amongst the prettiest wild plants to encounter. This salt loving coastline plant also frequents the loose stone shingle outside Rhynvella Beach, its natural habitat. The friendly Sea Mayweed is a member of the Daisy Family, and is a perennial non scented plant. Pineapple Weed, which mainly grows locally in loose gravel areas is a closely related species but lacks the ray florets of Mayweed. Sea Mayweed should not be confused with Ox-eye Daisy, which is a taller erect plant with a different leaf structure and the petals do not fold back. Oxeye Daisy is not common in the Peninsula, but occurs South of Carrigaholt.

ROCKY, STONY AND SANDY BEACHES

Shingle beach at Ross provides interesting shape texture and formation.

There is interest and abundance on the lower shore

Sea Beet (*Beta vulgaris maritima*) at Ross Beach

Sea Beet frequents Ross Beach in small quantities living above the tide line in loose beach shingle. A densely leaved fleshy plant with leaf shape varying from oblong to diamond shaped, dark rich green and waxy, Sea Beet sprawls itself over the loose beach stones, in full exposure to sun, rain and perhaps a run over from a high tide. Loving these salt laden conditions, Sea Beet, is a wild ancestor of vegetables, such as Beetroot, and Sugar Beet. The leaves are deemed to have a pleasant texture raw or cooked, and it is also known as Wild Spinach. The leaves are best eaten in Spring when young.

The flower heads of Sea Beet are green in a long dense spike flowering from July to September. Cosmetic scientific research has been carried out on Sea Beet, which is rich in anti-oxidants, and extracts from the plant are deployed in anti-ageing cosmetic formulae. French cosmetic companies have also employed extractions from the humble looking Sea Beet, in shampoos and conditioners, because it is said to revive dull, damaged hair restoring brightness and volume. Such a resourceful plant on our doorstep!

On the roadside shingle at Ross Beach, one meets a dense colony of the stout and robust Curled Dock. Growing to approx one metre, this tall 'seeded' looking plant has long oblong leaves that are curled and serrated at the edges. A member of the Dock family, I have been aware of this plant from a very young age, when its leaves were often compressed against my skin after having a bleeding injury or been stung by a nettle. Acting as an astringent, the leaf would stop the bleeding or relieve the itchy symptoms of the nettle sting. However, the Dock, was not a favoured plant of farmers, because its leaves are poisonous to cattle and sheep.

Another tall and somewhat ragged plant growing on the stony way sides and inside the beach at Ross is the Perennial Sow Thistle. This plant can look more like a Dandelion than a Thistle, because of the similarity of its flower head, its hollow stem and a leaf that bears some resemblance to that of the Dandelion. However, unlike the Dandelion, this plant is tall (to 1 meter tall) and highly branched. It exudes a milky juice from its stems when cut. The stems are ribbed and strong, the leaves are mainly arranged alternately around the middle of the plant, where they clasp the stem. Flowers - July-August.

Curled Dock *(Rumex crispus)*

Perennial Sow Thistle *(Sonchus arvensis)*

Hedge Bindweed (*Calystegia sepium spp roseata*)

Bittersweet (*Solanum dulcamara*) at Ross Beach

Hedge Bindweed is a dense mat-forming creeping plant with fleshy arrow shaped leaves and it can be seen on the top of Ross Beach on the far Eastern side where it basically knits the beach stones together. This particular sub-species is rare except on Western and Northern Coasts. It has an attractive large stripy pink and white trumpet shaped flower, 3-5cm in diameter which are singular at the end of flowering stalks which flower from June to September. The plant which likes to inhabit coastal areas could be used as a natural deterrent of coastal erosion. Very similar to the Sea Bindweed but leaf shape differs.

We discovered the distinctive but poisonous Bittersweet at Ross Beach in Summer 2010. Growing on the loose shingle above the tide line, it is densely crowded with large alternating leaves along its red tinged stem. Its unique flower of deep purple and rich golden yellow makes the plant easy to identify. Flowering from early May, the flower consists of five pointed purple petals, a deeper purple centre, with a ring of bright yellow-green dots at the petals base. There is a protruding yellow column of stamens. After flowering it produces red oval berries. Also recorded at Rhynvella Beach.

ROCKY, STONY AND SANDY BEACHES

Rock Sea Spurrey (*Spergularia rupicola*)

Sea Milkwort (*Glaux maritima*)

Mainly growing out of gravelly rock crevices, we have recorded several sightings of Rock Sea Spurrey, mainly at the Bridges of Ross shore. A pretty and delicate plant, it has oblong fleshy leaves growing in a dense branched mat, with very pretty, delicate and small five petalled soft pink/lilac flower heads. Tucked unobtrusively into the rock crevices, one wonders what it feeds on. A member of the Campion Family, Rock Sea Spurrey flowers from May to August.

Growing in damp salty gravelly sand, near the serrated outcropped rock at Ross Beach is where James and I found the only habitation of Sea Milkwort that we have recorded in the Loophead Peninsula. The fleshy creeping and ascending plant with soft pink flower heads with deeper pink centres was practically camouflaged against its mottled grey surroundings of gravelly, broken shell infused sand, when we discovered it in 2010. This tiny plant, with dense oblong fleshy leaves flowers in early Summer and the above ground perennial herb dies off in the Autumn. Although not widely known for any medicinal properties, the Haida (indigenous people of British Columbia, Canada and Alaska) use the root of this plant as a sleeping medication, and also during the birthing process to relax the mother at the right time. Sea Milkwort is a coastal plant and can be found in damp salty habitats, like salt marshes, and marine mud.

Lichen-rich rocks dominate in the Splash Zone

Abundance of Plantains

There is both variety and abundance of plantains, salt marsh grasses and sedges growing on the gravelly salt marsh conditions at Ross beach, which, when mingled with the Sea Milkwort, Sea Mayweed, Silverweed and other flora provide for an interesting rummage on a fine Summer day.

Sea Club Rush (*Bolboschoenus maritimus*) at Ross Beach

ROCKY, STONY AND SANDY BEACHES

The withdrawn low Spring tide at Rhynvella Beach on the Shannonside lays bare a varied cache of normally hidden species and formations of the sea bed.

Spear-leaved Orache (*Atriplex prostrata*) in flower

RHYNVELLA BEACH

The Shannonside beach of Rhynvella is the last mixed stony and sandy beach on the Shannon before it flows into the Atlantic Ocean. Although noticeably tame by comparison with its Northern counterpart on the Atlantic side, there is still a very strong ocean influence, which is evident in stormy and high tides, its rounded stony seashore and the salt loving plants that like to exist here. The shingled roadsides at Rhynvella are species-rich with a floral footprint that is unique to this particular zone. On the shingled roadsides, one can find an abundance of wonderful Wild Carrot, Common Scurvy Grass, Red Bartsia, Wild Mallow, Teasel, Spear-leaved Orache, Frosted Orache, Curled Dock, Perennial Sow Thistle, Sea Mayweed and Sea Beet. On the inside of the beach there is the pretty Sea Rocket, Bittersweet and Spear-leaved Orache.

Spear-leaved Orache can be found in both an erect and sprawling format on the shingled beaches of both Ross and Rhynvella, its preferred habitation in the Peninsula. Widely variable in its composition, the russet coloured spear-shaped leaves provide a very attractive foliage that will draw you to this plant. Earlier in the Season these leaves are green. Its dense flower spikes of tiny pink flowers bloom from July to October.

Spear-leaved Orache (*Atriplex prostrata*) at Rhynvella

ROCKY, STONY AND SANDY BEACHES

The young Common Scurvy plant

Common Scurvy Grass (*Cochlearia officinalis*) at Rhynvella

On late April and May trips to Rhynvella Beach, one is met with full flourishing Common Scurvy Grass, with its mass of delicate four petalled white flower heads with yellow stamens beaming and beckoning the passer-by. By far the greatest showing of this plant in the Peninsula, Common Scurvy Grass, which is in fact a member of the Cabbage Family, has its settlement right outside the re-enforced and gabion walls mingled in the shingled roadside. It is a low growing and sprawling plant with succulent kidney-heart-shaped leaves, that are very rich in Vitamin C. Although, the older leaves are bitter tasting, baby leaves collected in Spring are much more palatable and have a peppery taste. Common Scurvy Grass is found right across the world, from the Faroe Islands to New Zealand, where its mineral rich properties are hailed and where it is employed as a substitute to fresh vegetables, when none are available. Because of its richness in Vitamin C, it was used by sailors, to enrich their diet, and prevent the onset of scurvy disease, hence the name of this plant. Growing close to the seashore, or up-river where the influence of the sea, still persists, Common Scurvy Grass also appears in smaller settlements at the Bridges of Ross mingled in the Red Fescue.

Sea Rocket (*Cakile maritima*) at Rhynvella Beach

Sea Rocket is a delicate pretty plant to encounter among the loose beach stones at Rhynvella. With just a small number of plants occupying this beach, and the only location that I have found Sea Rocket in the Peninsula, Sea Rocket actually prefers a more sandy location than that provided here. It has rich green glossy, succulent and deeply lobed leaves which can be eaten in salads or cooked when the leaves are young in Springtime, providing a rich source of Vitamin C. The flower head is four petalled ranging in colour from soft pink/lilac to white, fading with age. The plant is low growing and sprawling with a very deep tap root, that helps hold it in position against a robust tide or strong winds, in its normal habitat, the sandy shore. The ripened dried fruits of Sea Rocket are carried off in tidal flotsam and can arrive and set down new roots on another beach anywhere. Sometimes it can be buried by heavy sand deposits but it responds by growing higher, its fleshy leaves at all times storing moisture to survive through drought periods and dry sands/soil. A member of the Cabbage family, it has a sweet delicate perfume and it is worth bending to catch the wonderful scent.

With almost cacti like qualities, the stiffly and prickly Wild Teasel occupies some waste ground in the direct vicinity of Rhynvella Beach, and hence mentioned in this section, to allow the reader combine the search for this plant with the other plants of the Rhynvella Beach area. Wild Teasel can grow to over a metre in height, is biennial, and is highly distinguishable with its sculpted bracts arising from beneath its large egg-shaped flower head, heading towards the sky. The egg shaped flower head provides an exceptional ringed display of tiny mauve-pink flowers. Its tall, stout, and erect stem provides a sense of architectural pomposity as it stands out from the crowd. This plant is a major attraction for bees, butterflies and other insects, and Goldfinches feed on its seeds. In times past, the spiny heads of Teasel were used to comb woollen cloth. I have only encountered Wild Teasel at Rhynvella and it is by no means common in Ireland, but much more common in the UK.

Wild Teasel is a most dramatic plant, and it will consume your undivided attention when you come upon it. One is not invited to touch its prickly stem, bract or its spiny honeycomb-like flower head. Its flowering rings of mauve flowers develop from June onwards. Its height can be quite variable and James and I have discovered lower growing Teasel on the waste ground at the Western side of Rhynvella Beach. The spent plants that have had their biennial time expired can hang around for a time if undisturbed.

Above and Below Wild Teasel(*Dipsacus fullonum*) near Rhynvella Beach.

Competing with the Teasel for height and architectural flamboyance is the much softer to the touch and rarely found species of the Babington's Leek. This plant can be found in the Western direction from Rhynvella Beach growing from inside a ditch, but reaching far over it, therefore presenting the walker and passer-by with a full viewing of its exquisite flower head. This relatively sheltered location near Rhynvella Bay is the only one where I have discovered Babington's Leek in the Western Loophead Region. Apparently it can also be found on the Aran Islands, and around Galway Bay, but is otherwise rare in Ireland and Britain. As the crow flies, neither location is far away. It grows near coasts but not in direct maritime exposure. It is a native plant to the British Isles. The plant which grows from a bulb, to approximately 1.5 metres tall, is erect with long linear leaves which flop downwards. At the top of its rounded erect stem, forms a flower head consisting of bulbils which are covered over in a soft white papery sheath and ending in a long tall spike. These covered flower heads can be seen from early June. This reminds me of a plant that wishes to unveil its flower head as a piece of artwork, at an exhibition opening. It is probably a protection sheeting keeping its bulbils together and away from insects or other predators, or from the sun. Whatever its purpose, when the sheath unfolds the flower head beneath, one is left in awe of the magnificent formation and delicate detail, with pedicels of unequal lengths supporting small and delicate soft pink/purple flowers reaching higher into the sky. This flower head is a unique work of natural art.

Babington's Leek, can be grown from the bulbils of its flower head, which will take a few years to reach a fully grown plant. This is a plant that was used in times past as a garlic like flavouring ingredient. The leaves and flower head are edible, but for me, much too rare and beautiful to eat.

The rare & beautiful Babington's Leek *(Allium babingtonii)* at Rhynvella

James and I discovered a small colony of the densely leaved spiky flowered Red Bartsia growing on the Northern roadside in front of Rhynvella Beach in Summer 2011. At this location it was growing in the midst of Sea Mayweed, Perennial Sow Thistle, Frosted Oraches and general grasses, which thrive through the Shannon driven loose beach stones that have found their home here too. The flowers which are two-lipped, light magenta shaded, and providing a dense showing on a long reddened spike were in bloom in August when we first recorded the plant. A member of the Figwort Family, and related by botanical identification with the Eyebrights, Speedwells and Foxglove, Red Bartsia is partly parasitic fastening itself onto the roots of grasses around it and drawing water and minerals from those roots. In times past, Red Bartsia, was used as a cure for toothache, its botanical name 'Odont' is the Greek for tooth.

Red Bartsia (*Odontites vernus*)

Common Mallow (*Malva sylvestris*) at Rhynvella Beach

But far more conspicuous by virtue of its sweet rose-pink colouring, and standing out against a back drop of muted greens and stone greys in this section of Rhynvella Beach, just across the road from the beach itself, the Common Mallow, draws on one's attention. The relatively large flowers have five petals that are veined in a deeper shade of pink. With its palmately lobed and shallow toothed leaves, hairy to the touch, Common Mallow forms a loosely clustered flower display with individual flower stalks (pedicels). This plant is not common in this region, the garden varieties of the Mallow family being much more common. Common Mallow, which is a much more common plant in Southern Europe, is known and used by folk communities as a herbal medicine. In parts of Southern Italy for example, its panacea as a cure all is declared in a local saying 'La Malva, da ogni mal'ti salva' (The Common Mallow saves you from every disease!) In such communities, it is used as a cure for colds and flu, stomach ache, toothache and other diseases. Scientists of today are re-looking at these remedies in taking a new approach towards combating drug resistant bacterial infections.

Wild Carrot

Deriving delight from the sumptuous splendour of the Wild Carrot, generates for me the most pleasing of moments in my wild flower journeys. Being stopped in my tracks by its exquisite formation and delicate detail, words do not adequately describe the floral sensation that is the Wild Carrot. Its habitat at Loophead is mostly contained within the roadside just across from Rhynvella Beach where it mingles the Shannon landed stones, and other vegetation, easily outshining its competitors. It can also be found in small quantities on the inner beach edges at Ross Beach in a sunny disposition near the moor top. Not surprisingly alternatively titled 'Queen Annes Lace', the Wild Carrot is revered in folklore and in herbal medicine and in wild gourmet cooking. The Sea Carrot is a sub-species of this plant.

Wild Carrot *(Daucus carota)*

The Wild Carrot is a highly variable plant, and depending on the vegetative support and atmospheric conditions around it, one can encounter this plant growing to one metre tall, but not at Loophead. The tiny flowers that combine to make up the umbel are normally a soft creamy colour with tinges of pink and a central pink or red floret - one of its distinguishing features. Its leaves are finely divided like that of the Carrot. These lush green leaves grow alternatively on a ribbed stem that is often rough and hairy to the touch. Flowering from June to August, another distinguishing feature are the drooping green feathery bracts just beneath the umbel. This decadent lace-like plant is employed in herbal medicine as a decoction or an infusion, and is associated with assisting such ailments as diabetes, soothing the digestive tract, and stimulating the removal of waste from the kidneys. It is also used in making jelly and confectionary. For me, the Wild Carrot is a testament to the glory of nature.

The gently winding narrow road at Kilballyowen unfolds a pathway to unrivalled wayside blossoming from late July.

Chapter 5 - Waysides, Verges, Hedgerows & Drains

Generating lyrical movements in an enchanted incandescent environment, the Montbretia, fills the senses and the landscape with its fiery colour from mid July to mid September, before the rusting of its long linear oxide green leaves into Winter's wilderness. This wild flower, who purists castigate as being a 'Garden Escape' has naturalized itself in the Loophead hedgerow environment for at least the past fifty years, bringing with it, dazzling colour and a spirit of non-restraint.

No boundary shall restrain your flourish,
for you will elegantly sway your petals beyond,
be undisturbed, if a little inconvenienced
by the walls and wires
that strive to hold you in 'your' place -
but you have the freedom of the Universe,
there are no laws prohibiting
your random flourish, your fertile beauty,
you may conquer, enthrall, mesmerize -
FREEDOM BLOSSOMS!

At Loophead, the waysides, verges, hedgerows and drains together present the greatest variety of wild flora in the region. After spending several Winter months, in natures lifeless, withered, withdrawn state, the first welcoming signs of Spring present themselves with the mid - March flowering of wrinkle leaved Primroses, firstly hidden in well shaded bush scrub, before exposing themselves widely at every crossroads junction, high up and low down on the ditches, and even down the muddy vertical cliff sides at Ross. Together with spiny ever-green Furze, scarcely bespeckled at this time with yellow flowers, Primroses herald the first sign of Spring's verdant and colourful revival,

which continues unabated thereafter. The verges become lush with fresh growing grasses, The Sally Bush's buds expand and decorate its tall smooth stems. Last years mingled and mangled dead growth gives way to new vegetative flourishment, and a March into April Spring flush of Dandelions. Colouring the now greening fields with their brilliant sunshine yellow, the Dandelions are both under-appreciated and under-estimated in their value to the natural world. A tiny blue flower known as the Common Dog Violet also flowers sporadically along the ditches at this time.

As the month of May unfolds the delicate, short run flower that is the Cuckoo Flower raises its delicately shaded soft pink-lilac colour generously amongst the blades of grass, but mostly in the fields, which can be fully viewed from the roadway. Now too Ribwort Plantain, the Tufted Vetch and the Red Clover are beginning their long flowering show, and as well as being present on the waysides, they have the privilege of being wanted in farmers fields to feed the livestock with their nutrient rich fodder. Lucky plants! On wet waysides and in wet marshy fields, one cannot miss the tall, strongly built Yellow Flag (Feileastram). The known Irish names of many plants and seaweeds lingers and are more frequently used than their English counterparts, because until recently, this was a Gaelthacht. However, the names of most plants are not locally known. Little plants such as Herb Robert are present on the more sheltered ditches inland while the magenta hues of Fumitory holds its position on grassy verges.

June calls in a myriad of tall flowering plants like the Buttercup, the Ragged Robin, Babington's Leek, Wild Privet, Cow Parsley, Hogweed, Valerian, Spear Thistle, Creeping Thistle and Marsh

WAYSIDES, VERGES, HEDGEROWS AND DRAINS

Thistle, with a greater all round display at the end of the month than at the beginning. Higher up on the Hedgerows, we have the floral artwork that is the sweetly scented Honeysuckle together with Bindweed. The scarce Oxeye Daisy also puts on a show on the hedgerows south of Carrigaholt.

However, it is July and August that the rich floral bearing on the waysides, verges, hedgerows and drains seeks your undivided attention. Purple Loosestrife, Montbretia, Meadowsweet, Greater Willow Herb, Knapweed, Wild Angelica, St John's Wort, Ragwort (Buachalán) Fleabane and fruiting Bramble vie for your attention.

Infiltrating the air with your flamboyant scents,
colouring the now high meadows
with shades of orange, pink, purple and cream,
you carelessly sway
in a soft silken sun-drenched breeze,
amongst the green and golden blades of hay.
How magical
this careless bounty of beauty,
that flourishes, without labour,
to inflate, our oft trodden,
misplaced sense of beauty.
Please Stay!

Expect the unexpected - an optical illumination - luscious vegetation brimming with vibrant energy and movement.

Winter's wilderness provokes a sense of abandonment.

Christmas Day - Killballyowen - Walk through the Snow

Looking through the window panes
on this bright Christmas mid-morn,
A white landscape beguiles the senses, stretching far and wide,
unique in my lifetime and in my mother's nine decades
in this coastal habitat.

...So with my pure woollen knitwear,
and my best gripping walking shoes,
I set foot on an unsure roadway, slowly testing its slipperiness
before confidence sets in.
The snowfalls of the past days have nobly
transformed the entire landscape
enhancing its textures and highlighting the dips, hollows,
peaks and clumsy growth on Winter's fields.
The now lifeless umbels and florets of Summers blossoms
delicately spun in Winter's most decadent purest lace.
And oh what lace, no Victorian ladies could string this majestic detail,
nor Renaissance sculptor in fifty years detailed sculpting
could spring this Winter's overnight surprise,
these white stalks in noble bow,
tall branches in delicate sparkle covered. -
A Christmas gift of purity in nature's noble act
of transformation lingering momentarily or two.

Trundling slowly on the snow cast road,
where only one man and dog has been before,
and the toothed tyres of a large tractor
laid its design on the deeper snow.
A sense of Attenborough's tundra sets in, abandoned lifeless fields,
and a distant cow from a byre moos for her morning fodder
or some other need.

I pass the only inhabited homestead where that dog lingers,
and with whom I made friends in the July days of festive hedgerows,
and so I pass without a trace, but suddenly he is near to foot
in a frenzied barking rage,
irritating the entire landscape,
threatening its lasting purity,
until finally he disappears.

Then I cast to the sun noting its white dazzling rays
before I blink at the blue sky and 'tis when I search for the clouds,
to determine their prominence, that a different story emerges.
I see a jet with its white trail of smoke, and then further east
I notice two more,
then a fading streak of an earlier one and when I look closer
the remnants of many more.
From here on in, I study the sky, as I read
of the rampant rush of the various jets
to New York and Boston where Christmas Day has not yet started.
Flying capsules of living beings, capsules of cock-tailed emotions,
delayed by snowfall's downfall to mankind.
And I celebrate their momentary company
in this abandoned roadway.

This image instills hope and inner ecstacy,
the hope of reunion and celebration, just above me in the sky.
For a while I remember my young sick friends,
As I consider the hope that radiates within this mid-morn walk,
under a bright blue sunshine sky,
a healing hope, a joyful hope, pure hope within.
A slight slip of the foot brings me back to the snowbound ground,
where a cuddly curvy song thrush skips dandily from bush to bush,
just there, in search of Winter crusts.
Birds are flying today, but not in great abundance,
and no more have I seen,
than the fifteen or so jet streams now counted.
In this peaceful lowly landscape, no one save I stirs today,
a magical walk on a white lacy way.

(2010)

WAYSIDES, VERGES, HEDGEROWS AND DRAINS

Spring in full Furze swing - this narrow Fodera-Loophead road is single-sidely covered in Furze blooms .

The Furze, accompanied by its rich Celtic folklore, occupies hedgerows, ditches and waste scrub land throughout the Peninsula. The temperate coastal climate allows for some early flowering, and one can find this shrub presenting blooms as early as November. The long flowering Season of Furze continues into May, colouring and clothing the landscape with its warm yellow tones, bringing with it the symbolism of the power of the Sun. Furze, also known as Gorse, is in fact associated with the Celtic Sun God, Lugh - the God of light and genius, and with the Spring Equinox, where it is seen to be one of the only plants in full bloom at this time. Furze gives inspiration to Spring and Autumn Festivals, including the Celtic Festival of Lugnasdagh, in Brittany on August 1st, known as *'The Festival of the Golden Gorse'*

Furze is a member of the Pea family, is a perennial evergreen, a spiny, highly branched shrub, growing to no more than two metres. With its prickly needles, and its dense vegetative form, it is often viewed as having protective powers, and makes a natural protective hedgerow and barrier. Chopped up branches were sometimes placed on vegetable beds to keep birds and mice away from newly planted crops.

The flowers have been used to make a yellow dye, and were used to add both flavour and colour to Irish whiskey, while being used in beer making in Denmark.

Both Culpepper and Pliny the Elder had their view on the Furze, with Culpepper stating that a 'decoction made with the flowers was good to open obstructions of the spleen', whilst Pliny the Elder, stated that branches were placed in streams to collect gold dust, from the water, then dried and burned and gold could be collected as tiny nuggets from the ash!

Furze *(Ulex europaeus)*- an ancient, powerful symbol of nature

Throughout the Centuries, Furze has been employed as livestock fodder - it being high in protein, as fuel for the ovens of bakeries - catching fire easily due to the high concentration of oil in its leaves, to banish fleas - with its seeds sodden and shook around the house, as a medicine for children suffering from Scarlet Fever, as a protector of animals in the Winter Season, in Celtic Beltane bonfires, and in homeopathy, as a symbol of hope and encouragement. Inspiring poets and writers along the way, the Furze is a powerful and ancient symbol of nature.

Primrose (*Primula vulgaris*) Kilballyowen ditch

The first notions of Spring's arrival can be unobtrusively tucked behind the withered stems of Bramble and grasses from last years crop. As if for its own safety, this early and hidden little Primrose seems in need of the protection of such vicious thorns. As the season progresses, however, the Primrose gladly shows its soft yellow, deeper yellow centered, five lobed wheel shaped flower all along the roadsides, ditches and vertical cliff faces. Beneath its flower head it has a woolly calyx tube and a long woolly flower stalk as if to keep warm. It forms a basal rosette of obovate shaped wrinkled leaves.

From my younger days, I recall being drawn to the colourful displays of the Primrose on the muddy vertical cliff faces at Ross. To survive in this environment suggests that the Primrose is a salt tolerant plant. It was very tempting for me as a child, to climb down this grassy vertical bank to collect some of these pretty flowers, which I did. The primrose can also be found in places such as woodland, and performs well across several habitats and soil types. There are many cultivated variants of this plant, which are planted in Spring gardens.

Dandelion *(Taraxacum/officinale agg.)*

Nothing infuses my being with the enthusiasm of Spring more than the large sunny/lemon radial florets of the Dandelion occupying entire fields in their dense sunshine colour.

'Perhaps I'll wait for the Spring Parade of Dandelions
through the Spring grassed fields,
their bright yellow florets encircling me
in renewable creative energies each year'

These highly under-rated plants are like nature's natural and visual tonic. Firstly they feed the senses, bringing hope and expectation of the Spring and Summer, finally nailing the greyed Winter hues. Secondly, with their deep tap root, they draw up nutrients from the soil for other shallow rooting plants, including, grass to obtain, at the start of the new growth Season. Attractive to pollinating insects and releasing ethylene into the atmosphere, which helps fruit to ripen, the Dandelion, which is vigorously common across habitats deserves its respect. Perhaps one of its greatest uses lies in human herbal medicine, where it was first written about in these terms by Arabian physicians back in the tenth Century. The main herbal values of the plant center around its use as a 'purifier' of the liver, kidneys and blood. It is seen as a general stimulant to the system. The leaves and the roots are the parts used. Dandelion tea is widely available in wholefood stores. A member of the Daisy family, its main flowering flush occurs between March and April.

In the mostly saline and wind exposed ditches and hedgerows of Loophead, Herb Robert is not a common resident, preferring instead to occupy mostly sheltered hedgerows on the inner roads away from direct ocean influences. It is here near Doonaha, on the Shannonside, that I have found Herb Robert, in full russet and pink glory. A most attractive plant, in sun exposure, it also likes woodland habitats and shaded walls and ditches, where a much greener version of the plant can be found. Herb Robert is a member of the Geranium family, with much divided feathery bright green leaves, russet in sun exposure, and a soft powdered pink five petalled flower head. Its stems are also deep russet in colour. It has a long flowering Season, and is often one of the first flowers to spot in April. Herb Robert can still be flowering in November. It has a long historical background associated with it and it has been used in Herbal medicine as a remedy for toothaches.

Common Dog Violet (*Viola riviniana*)

As if to counteract the lack of courage of Herb Robert to be exposed to the harsh conditions at Loophead, Common Dog Violet, exposes its minute self to the elements on open ditches from March. This tiny plant will not beckon your attention, but it will reward you, on finding it, with its pretty five petalled lavender- violet shaded, slightly Pansy-like flower head, its dense and shiny heart shaped leaves, and its bowed arched stem. Its petals too are veined in a deep violet shade, to guide and attract insects to its nectar. When floral sightings are meagre at this time, Common Dog Violet, which is a member of the Violet Family, is like a passive, miniature messenger, advising the viewer of what is yet to unfold. Common Dog Violet can be found high on exposed ditches throughout the Peninsula from March to June, and is common throughout Ireland.

Herb Robert (*Geranium robertianum*) at Doonaha

Lesser Celandine *(Ranunculus ficaria)*

Cowslip *(Primula veris)*

The greening and yellowing hues of Spring continue with sightings of other pretty Spring flowers, including the Lesser Celandine and Cowslip. Although neither plant produces a profuse showing in the Peninsula, they are likely to request your attention from the grass verges and drains on the roadsides.

Lesser Celandine is a creeping and ascending plant, with heart-arrow shaped glossy deep green leaves with singular flowers at the end of long stalks. A member of the Buttercup family, the flower head normally consists of eight shiny bright lemon-yellow petals, which fade to white with ageing and sun exposure. Liking damp soils, we have found Lesser Celandine on the road verges on the Moneen-Kilbaha road the Kiltrellig road and at Kilballyowen graveyard flowering from March to May.

Another rare display is that of the Cowslip, a closely related member of the Primrose family. Like the Primrose it has wrinkled oblong leaves forming a basal rosette. A long singular woolly flower stalk supports a clustered flower head of drooping golden yellow cup like flowers at the end of long calyx tubes. Having only found these pretty flowers along the Kilbaha roadside, their existence in the Western Loophead region appears scarce.

Sticky Mouse-ear (*Cerastium glomeratum*)

Cuckoo Flower (*Cardamine pratensis*)

Both the Sticky and Common Mouse-ear are amongst the many members of the Campion family that inhabit the Loophead Region. Other members include the Common Chickweed, Stitchworts and Common Whitlow Grass. Other than the Common Chickweed, none are overly abundant. I first encountered the Sticky Mouse-ear while on an early April walk with James some years ago, in a damp field. Its unfamiliarity to me, caused a long delay in its identification. Sticky Mouse-ear is an erect plant with paired ovate densely hairy leaves growing along its branching stem, which is also hairy. The terminal flower head is tightly populated with tiny five-petalled white flowers, each petal notched. Common Mouse-ear is a more sprawling plant, which I have discovered mostly in low vegetation near the sea or on road margins, with deeply notched five petalled flower heads that are loosely clustered.

After the wonderful flush of Dandelions have departed the growing young meadows and fields, the softly shaded lilac/soft pink to white tinged Cuckoo Flower begins its annual showing from late April. Its abundance will flourish in May, the time of our traditional May Altar to the Blessed Virgin, and this flower will hold its place in the floral display at the Altar. Also known as Lady's Smock or Mayflower and a member of the Cabbage Family, it has a basal rosette of leaves consisting of several leaflets. Its stem is normally straight and upright, growing to approximately 30cm with few branches at the end of which form stalked flower clusters of delicate refreshing four petalled flowers with soft mustard stamens. Much folklore surrounds the Cuckoo flower, it being directly associated with the return and singing of the Cuckoo. Its young leaves and flower heads are edible. The female Orange Tip Butterfly lays its eggs singularly on the flower heads of this plant.

WAYSIDES, VERGES, HEDGEROWS AND DRAINS

Honeysuckle (*Lonicera periclymenum*)

The exquisite flowers of the twining and climbing Honeysuckle are amongst the first each year to make a colourful impression on the taller hedgerows on the inner roads in the Peninsula. These large spectacular flowers which range in hue from rich yellows to deep crimsons and an entire pastel colour spectrum in between are show-stopping not only in their colour and formation but also in their sweet fragrance. A sturdy plant, its bending and winding stems are a russet-purple shade, with large untoothed oval shaped rich green leaves growing in pairs along the stems.

The flowers are in a whorl at the end of the stem, each one trumpet-shaped and two lipped with long protruding stamens, that are normally soft creamy yellow in colour. After its long flowering period which commences in early May, it produces red globular berries that are poisonous. On my Peninsula travels, I have found that the Honeysuckle prefers a more sheltered inner road habitat, where the surrounding vegetation of mostly brambles and grasses are tall and dense. To those of us in search of the true definition of beauty, a beauty that lifts Spirits, tickles visual excitement, fulfills its function in producing large amounts of sweet nectar, and inspires poets, artists, and nature lovers in its delicate formation, the Honeysuckle sets the standard. Also known as Woodbine and a member of the Honeysuckle Family of which there are over 180 different species worldwide, the native variety to Ireland is the *Lonicera periclymenum* as seen above.

WAYSIDES, VERGES, HEDGEROWS AND DRAINS

Ribwort Plantain (*Plantago lanceolata*)

Ribwort Plantain is a distinctive perennial plant that is widespread across all local habitats from the sea-front to the fertilized grasslands. A member of the well represented Plantain Family, like the Sea Plantain, it forms a basal rosette of dense lanceolate shaped leaves that are very palatable and nutritious to grazing sheep and rabbits. As a result of this it can be included in grass seed mixtures which accounts for its abundance in farmlands. The long single flowered stems are leafless, hairy and deeply furrowed. At the top of each flowering stem is a dense spike consisting of numerous tiny florets and surrounded by long whitish stamens. With a long flowering Season, commencing in April and continuing into the Autumn, there is a certain whimsiness about this plant that stirs attention, and it is one that has been much played with by children in games of the imagination.

With its source of calcium, phosphate, potassium, sodium, cobalt and copper trace elements, Ribwort Plantain is a valuable fodder plant, but it also has human medicinal uses being used as a tea that can treat coughs, with its young leaves providing astringent properties.

Full of the sensual spirit of freedom espoused by a flower that pitches itself amongst the long grasses and sways joyously in the dense tangled growth, the Ragged Robin inspires, art and poetry a plenty. This rare, but welcoming sight of the Ragged Robin amongst damp roadside vegetation, and in marshy distant fields, provides a pretty pink colouring in early June in the Peninsula's lands. A member of the Campion Family, it is tall growing to 40cm, with a sturdy ribbed stem and upwardly set narrow lanceolate leaves. The loosely formed clustered flower heads provide a 'torn and scruffy' looking pink flower with a dark ribbed calyx beneath it. A 'tear-away' free living plant that provokes joyousness.

Ragged Robin *(Lychnis flos-cuculi)*

Prickly Sow Thistle (*Sonchus asper*)

Wild Turnip (*Brassica rapa*)

I grew up at Loophead without ever noticing anything resembling a yellow coloured Thistle, always believing them to be various shades of pink. So it was with a certain disbelieving amazement, that I first spotted this 'Yellow Thistle' growing in a drain not far from my parents home some years ago. Eventually, confirming its identity with professional assistance, the Prickly Sow Thistle, is one of those robust, prickly plants that you do not touch. The flower heads look rather like those of a Dandelion, whilst the leaves and plant composition look very similar to those of a Thistle. Like both the Dandelion and the Thistle, Prickly Sow Thistle is a member of the Daisy Family. The standoffish leaves are deeply double toothed with spiny edges and clasp the stout hollow centered stem that exudes a milky sap when cut. Flower heads in a loose umbel flowering from early Summer.

Wild Turnip, growing in a roadside drain at Cloghaunsavaune, in recently disturbed soil, makes a rare, yet colourful appearance, in the Peninsula. This plant blooms at the same time as the Lesser Celandine and Common Dog Violet, and therefore provides an early season splash of colour. In other parts of Central and Eastern Europe and Central Asia, this plant is rampant, occupying large stretches of forest and river shores. It is sometimes cultivated for its oil content. It has stem clasping leaves, which differentiates this plant from other closely related species like The Wild Cabbage, Black Mustard and Rape, all members of the Cabbage Family. The loose umbel-like flower spike, of four petalled soft yellow flowers is flatter than that of the Rape or the Charlock, and the flower buds are below the flowers.

Red Clover (*Trifolium pratense*)

Common Sorrel (*Rumex acetosa*)

One of the few wild flowers to occupy grazing grasslands and meadows nowadays, the Red Clover holds its place because of its nutritional value to sheep and cattle. In fact the Red Clover is actively cultivated in farms for many reasons, including improving soil fertility, reducing the use of N fertilizer, and providing a high quality diet. The Red Clover provides pretty oval shaped deep magenta flower heads with oxide green trifoliate shaped leaves that have a white crescent shape mark. Because of their density and colour intensity, the flowering Red Clover can spectacularly occupy one's vision, and envelop the senses in the feel good being alive factor. Red Clover is also deemed to have rich herbal medicinal properties dating back several hundred years, and being deemed particularly useful in the purifying of the blood. It has also been deemed of benefit in menopausal and cancer treatments. A truly valuable, pretty, uplifting wild flower.

Common Sorrel is more like one of those wild plants that one knows exists, from the corner of one's eye, but it is not exciting enough to really beckon one's attention. More grassland, than wayside, the Common Sorrel is a member of the Dock Family, is a tall erect plant flowering in early Summer, with a branching flower head of densely populated small oxide red flowers. The leaves are long arrow shaped and shiny. Sorrel can be eaten in modest amounts in salad and soup, and has a sharp flavour, owing to the presence of oxalic acid. I have encountered Common Sorrel across several habitats at Loophead, including the taller grassier Moors at Loophead, atop ditches near Kilballyowen Graveyard, and commonly throughout the early Summer meadows.

Tunes of the Breeze

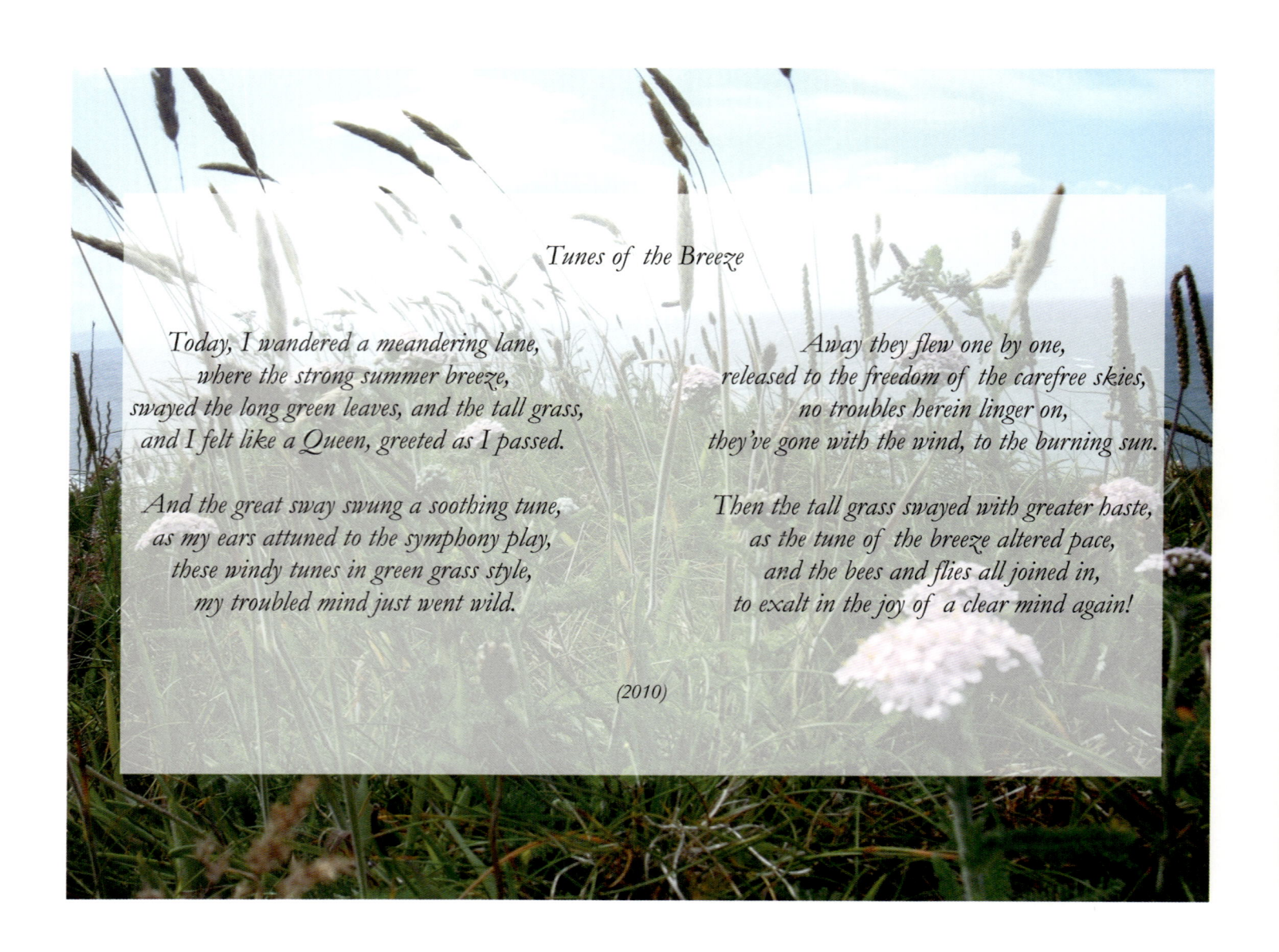

Today, I wandered a meandering lane,
where the strong summer breeze,
swayed the long green leaves, and the tall grass,
and I felt like a Queen, greeted as I passed.

And the great sway swung a soothing tune,
as my ears attuned to the symphony play,
these windy tunes in green grass style,
my troubled mind just went wild.

Away they flew one by one,
released to the freedom of the carefree skies,
no troubles herein linger on,
they've gone with the wind, to the burning sun.

Then the tall grass swayed with greater haste,
as the tune of the breeze altered pace,
and the bees and flies all joined in,
to exalt in the joy of a clear mind again!

(2010)

'The Bountiful Elder Tree'
by Mai Fennell (Mrs Mai Magner)

'Its uses as a cure are innumerable. Its leaves, bark and berries are all supposed to be good for something. Elder flower water is employed in perfumery, confectionery and has a very agreeable odour. An ointment is made out of the essential oil. The flowers are used also as a flavouring for jellies and the French pickle the flower buds like capers. It is the French too, who put layers of Elder flowers with casks of apples to improve the flavour of the apples.

Everyone knows Elderberry wine. There still exists a country habit of making syrup out of the berries for colds, sore throats and such. Certain species of the Elder provide cattle medicines from the bark. It is said that to scatter the floor of a granary with Elder boughs will keep away the rats and mice. The distilled water of the flowers is of much use to clear the skin from sunburn and freckles. It is also good for a headache. The leaves of flowers distilled in the month of May and the legs bathed in the water will take away ulcers and sores. Strip the blossoms from the stalk and cram them into a jug, fill with boiling water and cover. When cold, strain through muslin. It is very soothing for sore eyes. It is useful for a hair dye, the biting of serpents and mad dogs and for dropsies.'

(school assignment Kilbaha NS - 1934 - written in school copy)

Elder *(Sambucus nigra)* is a low growing shrub- small tree that mostly occupies corners of fields and boundary ditches in the Peninsula. A member of the Honeysuckle family, it is a densely leaved shrub with large opposite pinnate shaped leaves and an umble-like flat top flowerhead of tiny five petalled soft creamy flowers and produces a black edible berry. Decidious.

WAYSIDES, VERGES, HEDGEROWS AND DRAINS

Valerian (*Valeriana officinalis*)

Perhaps the tallest growing wild flower in the Peninsula, the soft delicate hues of the Valerian, accompany you for miles of roadway, where there are open drains with plenty moisture. Normally surrounded by dense vegetation, reeds, rushes and tall grasses, this metre plus plant has a strong round stem with paired pinnate leaves which get bigger towards the base. Leaflets are lanceolate, normally bluntly toothed.

The umbel-like fragrantly scented flower head consists of many tiny five lobed pinkish-lilac white flowers with protruding stamens.
 Valerian has been used as a medicinal herbal since ancient Roman and Greek times. Today Valerian is available from health stores, where it is offered for the natural treatment of insomnia. It can also be used as a sedative for nervous tension, hysteria, stress and cramps. The part of the plant that is harvested is the root, which, when dried contains an active oil ingredient that is extremely pungent. Valerian is a valuable herbal, and its flowers have been harvested for perfume making as long ago as the sixteenth century. In the Loophead Peninsula, Valerian is abundant along the Rhynvella Road, growing from open drains, and on marshy ground and waysides just beyond O' Shea's Cross on the road to Kilkee. It is much easier to locate during its flowering period starting in early Summer.

Burnet Rose (*Rosa pimpinellifolia*)

'The rose looks fair, but fairer we it deem for that sweet odour which doth in it live......
...Our own native roses blowing in some quiet country lane or clothing the dry sand banks with a spring-robe of beauty, and perfuming the whole atmosphere with their sweetness, as does the pretty little white-flowered Sand or Burnet Rose'

From the writings of Lord Byron
Anglo-Scottish Poet.

With its sweet scented fragrance, and its floppy five petalled creamy white flower with golden stamens, this attractive wild Rose, called the Burnet Rose, has a rare showing in the Peninsula wilds. It occupies a patch of hedgerow on the Kilballyowen-Rehy Road on the sunnier side of the road. Burnet Rose is common in the Burren, where its prickly existence on the limestone pavement is most handsome. The Burnet Rose likes seaside locations, and heath-clad hills inland. Its small oval leaflets are paired on its leaf stems and the central stem is exceptionally bristly. The singular flower heads give way to round dark purple to black fruit in the Autumn. These fruits are a rich source of vitamins and minerals, are sweet to taste, and have been used to make a fruity flavoured tea, far richer in vitamin C than oranges and blackcurrant. Many variants of the Burnet Rose have been cultivated in gardens.

Yellow Flag (*Iris pseudacorus*)

Creeping Buttercup (*Ranunculus repens*)

Locally known by its Irish name, 'Feileastram', this eye-catching, strong upright plant sets its base on wet marshy places, like low rush occupied fields, drains and field riverbanks. Because of the low flat lands that predominate the landscape at Loophead, meeting Feileastram here is common. Feileastram, which is a member of the Iris Family, is a wonderfully vibrant bright yellow flowering plant, with long sword shaped leaves, preferring open sunny conditions. Flowering from June to August, and normally found in patches which may occur because of the thick underground rhizomes spreading new shoots. A singular plant can in this way, cover a wide area. New plants also grow from seed dispersal. The Feileastram is not a favourite friend of the farming community, occupying lands, that cattle will not graze - because the Feileastram has poisonous glycosides, and is thereby avoided by animals. Nonetheless Feileastram is a visual treat.

The rich early Summer bounty of Meadow Buttercups herald the commencement of Summer in their glorious sunny hue. Infiltrating the now tall meadows, and swaying in the constant Peninsula breezes, when this buttercup flush beams up at a sunny blue sky beaming down, a magical magnetism unfolds, the buttercups pulling downward the sunny blue sky, whilst the sunny blue sky pulling upwards the sunny buttercups. This golden yielding and exchange between earth and sky visually and spiritually exhilarates the senses. The Buttercup Family is an expansive one, and examination of both flowers and leaves are often required to exactly identify the specie. Other members of this family described in this book include the Lesser Celandine and the Lesser Spearwort. Buttercups are poisonous to animals if eaten in the field, however they become harmless when harvested as hay.

Many members of the Carrot Family make an appearance on the Peninsula's waysides and hedgerows. For the most part these plants, which include, Wild Angelica, Cow Parsley, Hedge Parsley, and Hogweed prefer locations a little distance away from the front line shore, and are mostly found along the narrow inner roads. By far the prettiest is the Wild Carrot, and the newcomer to wild flora will need to spend some time studying leaf and flower systems to determine each one from the other. They are all umbellifers, and they are all coloured in various shades of whites or with soft creamy/pink tinges. Some members of this family are deadly poisonous, and therefore should not be eaten without expert knowledge and identification.

The tall robust Wild Angelica, appears singularly in dampish waysides, and in fields especially in more inland places like Kilballyowen and Rehy. It can grow to over a metre in height, has strong rounded tubular stems that are often tinged russet/purple, a feature similar to that of the deadly Hemlock. The leaves are two to three times pinnate, and the leaflets are toothed and oval to oblong in shape. The many rayed umbel shaped flower heads are densely populated with tiny pink/white flowers with petals curved inwards flowering from June to late August.

Wild Angelica was of immense ancient medicinal repute, and its name arises because of the fact that it was seen as a 'cure-all' for all epidemic diseases, and therefore had 'angelic' qualities. Culpepper for example declared ' the stalks or roots candied and eaten fasting, are good preservatives in time of infection; and at other times to warm and comfort a cold stomach ... The juice put into the hollow teeth, eases their pains!

Even though Wild Angelica does not beckon one's attention with its comparatively dull colouring, it does seek one's attention with its staidly yet solid up righteousness!

Wild Angelica (*Angelica sylvestris*)

A Sea of Purple Loosestrife adds vibrant colour to the landscape near the Church of the Little Ark

Bindweed (*Calystegia sepium*)

Wild Privet (*Ligustrum vulgare*)

This white Bindweed known as Hedge Bindweed, tends to inhabit the same upper hedgerow space as the Honeysuckle. It does however prefer the shadier hedgerows. It is a creeping and climbing plant with lush arrow shaped leaves and a large trumpet-bell shaped white flower. This plant climbs by circling its flexible stem around existing vegetation, choking them in the process. Because of its ability to spread and choke quickly, Bindweed is seen as an invasive unwelcome weed. This meshing and knitting of the hedgerows does however, lend itself to other clambering flowers like the Meadow Vetchling, and the Common Vetch.

Wild Privet is an attractive semi-evergreen shrub that I have found growing in Hedgerows or on the inside of the Hedgerow fence on occasion. It is a densely leaved shrub with lanceolate shaped paired leaves and a conical shaped flower head of soft tiny creamy scented flowers both of which are poisonous to humans. It flowers in early Summer. Wild Privet has been used as garden hedging, and in warmer temperate areas such as the coastal region of Loophead, it will retain its leaves over the Winter months. A member of the Olive family, after flowering it produces a round black shiny berry.

Cow Parsley (*Anthriscus sylvestris*)

Hedge Parsley (*Torilis japonica*)

Cow Parsley is a tall erect densely leaved plant that inhabits hedgerows and open fields in the area. The leaves are ferny and a lush green colour and the stout stem is ribbed. The plant is highly branched and like many other members of the Carrot Family, has an umbel of tiny soft creamy white flowers flowering from June to August. Cow Parsley should not be confused with Hogweed, which has very large divided leaves.

Hedge Parsley bears a greater resemblance to the Wild Carrot, and in true freedom fashion, this plant had set up home atop a ditch! This plant has tinges of light and dark pink in its flower head, and is more delicate and slender than the Cow Parsley. Widespread on waysides in the area.

The wild flowers of Loophead are at their most decadent colourful best from late July. Hedgerows upon hedgerows of luscious rich colours, purples, pinks, creams, blues, yellows and the fiery orange of the Montbretia ensure that this wonderful wild open hedgerow garden, that presents itself labour free, will encircle one in its floral charms. On the edge of the ocean, these bountiful hedgerows have inspired my art and poetry for the past decade. Within these hedgerows a hive of insect activity partakes, with flies, bees, butterflies, small birds and a myriad of tiny colourful insects, humming, buzzing, fluttering, flying, chirping, pollinating, collecting, whilst the constant fresh silken breeze sways every blade and floret. These blessings of nature are bestowed upon us, to give joy, lift the inner Spirit, show beauty, and when Winter comes, give hope of a Summer yet to bloom. One cannot experience this grace, by glancing and speeding past. These blooms will slow one down, so as to appreciate their true value one needs time to be directly in their midst, in an atmospheric, elemental, fresh environment that simply uplifts the Spirit.

One of my towering favourites is the July-August flowering Purple Loosestrife. Whorls of six petalled rich purple-magenta flowers, densely clustered in tall spikes sharing hedgerow space with other richly coloured species. These damp to wet marsh loving plants are very common in the Loophead Peninsula across various habitats, but always away from direct ocean exposure. The stalkless leaves are paired and lanceolate shaped and the stems are often deep red tinged. These plants begin their growth in Spring and one waits in patient expectation for their promised burst of colour. Purple Loosestrife can be found along all main roadsides as well as the narrow inner roads of the Peninsula where soil is moist.

Purple Loosestrife (*Lythrum salicaria*)

Another beautiful bushy tall (to one metre) occupant of the July -August hedgerows at Loophead is the Greater Willowherb. Not as conspicuous as the Purple Loosestrife, the pretty rich pink flowers with over-lapping and notched petals are bell shaped and singular at the end of long red tinged stalks. The leaves and stem are downy to the touch and the abundantly populated leaves appear in pairs, are stem clasping and are lanceolate shaped.

The Greater Willowherb brings verdant vegetative density to the hedgerows, portraying a sense of a well fertilized wild garden. This plant does like to set its creeping root on the damp roadside verge soils, that are abundant near drains in the area.

The Greater Willowherb is part of a large family of Willowherbs, and other less noticeable species exist in the Peninsula. like the Hoary Willowherb, and the Broad Leaved Willowherb, which can sometimes set root on the fresh earth of cultivated gardens. The Rosebay Willowherb, which has a splendid show stopping inflorescence has not been found present in the Peninsula wilds. The Greater Willowherb is also related to the pretty shrub Fuchsia, which also exhibits in the Peninsula.

This plant has also been called Codlins and Cream, and this title was associated with its cool delicate fragrance that emits when its top shoots are bruised.

In the Peninsula, the Greater Willowherb does not seek direct coastal exposure preferring the more sheltered non main, inner roadsides where it will grace your senses with its understated elegant appearance. Walking these quiet roads will bring one directly into its endearing company.

Greater Willowherb (*Epilobium hirsutum*)

As I sit and write this in the middle of flowerless January, my being is being transported back in time and to the Kilballyowen hedgerows where the rampant growth of one of my favourite Summer flowers, adds a calming fragrant dimension to the entire scene. These exquisite fluffy woody stemmed plants provide a gentle backdrop to the vibrant colours of the other occupants. In my photograph I have no desire to block out the other plants, because I believe that it is the bountiful tangled combination that exudes the sense of freedom, that sense that fills the inner being with elation, which returns to me in late Winter upon accessing the encapsulated memory. Meadowsweet is one of James' favourites, and we have collected little bunches to dry and make a fragrant pot pourri.

Meadowsweet is found abundantly throughout Ireland, mostly in damp marshy meadows and on river banks, A member of the Rose Family, it grows to approx one metre tall, has pinnate shaped leaves with two-five pairs of leaflets that are sharply toothed and oval in shape. These leaves are dark green on top and pale green and downy underneath. The woody stem is red-brown tinged. The flower head is a panicle (branched raceme) of tiny soft cream highly perfumed flowers that each have five petals and several protruding stamens.

Meadowsweet is of ancient Medicinal repute, and was sometimes referred to as 'nature's aspirin'. In 1652 Culpepper wrote that Meadowsweet 'helps in the speedy recovery from cholic disorders and removes the instability and constant change in the stomach'! Traces of Meadowsweet have been found in human remains in the UK dating back to the Bronze age, where it may have been used in a honey based drink. In more recent times, Meadowsweet, which contains salicylic acid, the main constituent in aspirin, has been used as a tea infusion, a capsule and been included in food preparation. It now appears to be used as a licensed medicinal tea in some countries for the treatment of colds and flu.

Meadowsweet (*Filipendula ulmaria*)

Scarlet Pimpernel (*Anagallis arvensis*)

Scarlet Pimpernel brings the attention of the eyes right down to the underfoot, because whilst all the tall floral vegetation is charming your senses at eye level, there are always delicate little plants at a low level that can easily be overlooked. Scarlet Pimpernel is by no means common in the Peninsula, and one is most likely to encounter it in a shingled road edge or low edge vegetation. This would need to be on a sunny day, as the normally creeping plant will close its pretty five petalled deep orange flower on the threat of rain, earning it the title of 'Poor Mans Barometer'! Scarlet Pimpernel which is a member of the Primrose Family has soft bright green hairless leaves which are in opposite pairs and are stem clasping in a pointed oval shape and are poisonous to animals. The little flower has been associated with ancient medicinal concoctions however, with Pliny the Elder and Culpepper writing about its various uses, the former suggesting its use in liver complaints, whilst both Culpepper and Gerard agreed that it was good for the eyes when mixed with honey and dropped into them! It is still used in a traditional herbal treatment in India today to treat gout.

WAYSIDES, VERGES, HEDGEROWS AND DRAINS

The Fiery Road - blazoned with Montbretia at Kilballyowen - Fiery yet peacefully co-existing in a quiet rural landscape.

Meadow Vetchling *(Lathyrus pratensis)*

For every level on the Summer verge or hedgerow, there is a flower that thrives at that level. Another scrambling but yellow coloured Vetchling is the Meadow Vetchling. This flower is strikingly like the Bird's-foot Trefoil at first glance, but one has to look closer to spot the paler green lanceolate shaped leaves, the tendrils used for latching and climbing onto taller vegetation, and the lighter lemon colour of the raceme flower heads. Both this Vetchling and Bird's-foot Trefoil are members of the Pea Family. One can encounter Meadow Vetchling at any level on the Hedgerow, depending on whether it prefers a scrambling and sprawling format to a climbing format. In all cases it is not as neat a formation as the Bird's-foot Trefoil, which has a neat mat forming appearance.

Fleabane, a member of the Daisy Family, can be found sporadically on the Peninsula's road margins and drains, and on waste disturbed grounds, growing to the more modest height of approx 60cm. It has downy oblong leaves that are stem clasping and alternate on a downy stem. This plant which flourishes on damp to wet soils, has a large golden yellow disk floret with short ray florets that are also golden yellow. Fleabane too has a history and it was once burnt in houses to rid the house of fleas, hence its name.

Fleabane *(Pulicaria dysenterica)*

'Floral Inclusion Zone Near Loophead'

*Rugged, lumpy terrain, an open space
un-toiled by human hands,
perhaps no man's land,
comes alive as
August announces her arrival.
Flourescent orange Montbretia
wave their oxide green leaves
in the constant breeze that exists
in this wild bedecked beautiful place.
And joined by the shades of pinks and purples
and the exotic creamy, fluffy
sweetly scented Meadowsweet
this has got to be Heaven
when looked down on
by a Heavenly blue sky!
(2006)*

Montbretia, the heart and soul, the fire and the energy, the feisty raw beauty, replenishes the Spirit with its magnificent free growing and free showing each year. Nothing colours the landscape more than the Montbretia during August's festive hedgerows at Loophead. Spreading itself through its bulbous runners, it makes no difference that it was so long ago a hybrid of garden origin that is said to have originated in South Africa. For my fifty years knowing this habitat, the Montbretia has been a main stayer on the verges of our roads. A member of the Iris Family, its long linear oxide green leaves are dense and always bowed, suggesting a welcoming demeanour. By far the personal favourite wild flower of both James and I.

Montbretia (*Crocosmia x crocosmiflora*)

Knapweed *(Centaurea nigra)*

Amphibious Bistort *(Polygonum amphibium)*

Another cheerful and colourful participant in the glorious Summer hedgerows on the inner Loophead roads is the Knapweed or Hardhead, the latter referring to its unopened hardened flower bud which is brownish in colour. A member of the Daisy family, with its flowers similar to the Thistle, Knapweed, takes root on road margins and ditches as well as meadow lands in the area. Unlike the Thistle, it is non prickly with stiff grooved stems, and oblong to linear shaped leaves. The flower head is fluffy and deep pink/magenta over the brown flower bracts and is singular at the end of flowering stems. Knapweed has been employed in Herbal medicine, and in Geoffrey Chaucer's day, it was used with pepper to stimulate the appetite. Culpepper wrote about its use in wound healing, by drinking a decoction of the dried root and seeds in wine, or applying it on to the wound surface!

Amphibious Bistort is less seen at Loophead, and one needs to carefully observe the dense hedgerows to find it. This member of the Dock family can be found either floating in water or on damp soils often near river banks. All parts of the Bistort plant have been used in Herbal Medicine, and in wild food foraging, the oval pointed leaves are bitter to taste, the root is rich in starch and can be eaten if steeped in water and then roasted. This has been a useful food in times of famine. Flowering from June to August. A close relation, the Red Shank, can also be found in drains near Rhynvella.

Sweet Flowers of Summer

Sweet flowers of Summer
you dance me through
your fields of golden blade,
in ethereal float, in light limb frenzy,
your whimsy moves,
your sweet air surrounds me,
like winds of change,
you bathe my senses
in waves of floral fragrance.

Through your silence you submit,
to other sounds of Summer,
yet I hear you calling me
with your cyme and umbel,
In a silent language so profound,
you calleth me, to showeth me
your sweeping beauty to define,
but you, my pretty one,
your secret silence is sublime.

Though rooted firmly in sodden soil,
your freedom blithely lingers,
through gorse and fen, moor and heath,
careless, weightless, nimble.
The birds and bees, breeze and moth,
spread you everywhere,
and so free to conquer as you will,
your seed grows wild, your Spirit free,
Trefoil, Rattle, Centaury.

But like us mere humans, you lie exposed,
threatened, by nature's forces,
through sparseness and flood,
ledge, crevice or coastal mud,
you bravely root and prosper
tuck yourself low, grow silken hairs,
succulent leaves by the pair,
deepen your root, strengthen your colour,
or simply latch onto your nearest neighbour!

(2011)

Creeping Thistle (*Cirsium arvense*)

Unlike other Thistles that inhabit the area, the Creeping Thistle, will normally be found in dense roadside shows, because of its creeping rooting system. The leaves of this plant are truly pernicious to the touch with their spiny wavy toothed edges. The flowers of Creeping Thistle are a soft lilac colour, much paler that those of the Spear or Marsh Thistle.

It may be difficult to find attraction in the Creeping Thistle, but no creation of nature is purposeless, and the Creeping Thistle Provides food for the Goldfinch and Linnet, its foliage is used by up to twenty species of moth and butterfly, and the root, stem and de-spined leaves are edible and nutritious to humans. The Creeping Thistle, which is a member of the Daisy Family, also provides a sort of natural wayside barrier in the same way as the Furze provides a taller protective barrier, and in so doing has the ability to keep certain animals away from field crops.

Marsh Thistle (*Cirsium palustre*)

Spear Thistle (*Cirsium vulgare*)

The Spear Thistle is the most noble of Thistles, with attractive defined features and a rich pink flower head atop globular shaped green spiny bracts. With its defensive demeanour, even the leaves are shaped like spear-heads and are spiny, but still less threatening than either the Creeping Thistle or the Marsh Thistle. The Spear Thistle grows singularly along roadsides and in waste ground in the Region, but not very common.

Meanwhile the Marsh Thistle, which prefers a wetter habitat, is a straggly looking plant by comparison. Its leaves are sparse and narrow, and prickly, it has a taller than broader orientation The Marsh Thistle can be seen sporadically on roadsides near drains and in wet meadows. Both Thistles are members of the Daisy Family.

The Thistle has earned its stripes as the national flower of Scotland, and folklore has it that this prickly, defensive plant was self employed during the reign of Alexander III, when the Vikings intent on invading and conquering Scotland, landed on the Coast of Largs at night to slay the Scottish clansmen. In order to move quietly under cover of darkness, they removed their shoes! The Scotsmen who were sleeping in a field were quickly awakened to the screaming, roaring Vikings who had set foot on the prickly Thistles! This gave them time to fend off the invaders and the Thistle has been hailed as the royal symbol of Scotland since the reign of James III in 1470.

Ragwort (*Senecio jacobaea*)

Ragwort, is a deeply disliked wild flower. This is because it is poisonous to cattle and horses, and spreads itself throughout farmland quite easily. One of our Summer jobs, when we were young, was to pick this plant by its root out of the fields. However, Ragwort prevails to this day and can densely occupy lands in its rich golden hue. The leaves of the Ragwort are magnificent, lace-like, rich green, deeply lobed leaves and its attractive flower head is branched and clustered with golden yellow daisy-like flowers. Ragwort is an attractive wild flower, flowering from July to September, and common across habitats but especially in poor neglected pastures. The Cinnabar Moth chooses Ragwort to lay its eggs on, and the resulting caterpillar eats its leaves, making this caterpillar poisonous to birds, but the stripey colouration of the Caterpillar is a warning colouration to birds and they ignore it.

Fuchsia (*Fuchsia magellanica*)

Fuchsia is a wonderfully distinctive flowering shrub that is a member of the Willowherb Family. Its glorious flowers remind me of a ballerina's dress, with four rich red rounded and pointed sepals on the outside and four deep purple petals (skirt-like) inside and eight protruding stamens. These flowers dangle downwards from long narrow flower stalks. In the Loophead Region, it can be as much a part of a cultivated garden, as part of a wild and tall hedgerow. I have mainly found it on the Rehy roadside. The glossy leaves are red veined in opposite pairs, toothed and oval shaped. The stems are woody. Its rich combination of colour and dense flowering format draws one to its spectacular beauty.

Such a magnificent shrub inspires artists, designers the world over. It has even lent its name to the colour Fuchsia. Fuchsia flower heads find their way into wallpaper, logos and other decorative designs. For me, having Fuchsia shrubs in our garden, inspired much game making with the 'ballerina' flower heads, when I was young!

WAYSIDES, VERGES, HEDGEROWS AND DRAINS

Bramble (*Rubus fruticosus*)

Bramble or Blackberry, with its thorny spiny stems is extensive and common on the taller hedgerows in the Peninsula. This flowering shrub blooms in early Summer with panicles of soft pink five petalled flowers, later giving way to a rich flourishment of green berries, which turn red and then black when ripe. One of nature's 'superfoods' the Peninsula is a prime destination for collecting these berries for jam-making, as the general low growth of the Region ensures the prominence of this scrambling shrub which is a member of the Rose Family.

Marsh Mallow (*Althaea officinalis*)

Marsh Mallow is now an exceptionally rare plant in the Irish countryside. These plants are growing out of a drain on the Ross/Cloghaunsavaune Road and they are the only ones that I have located in the Region. These plants feel velvet and intensely downy to the touch. The leaves are stalked and pale grey green in colour are oval to round in shape and somewhat folded and lobed. The flowers are five petalled pale lilac cup-like flowers with deep centres. It has a late flowering Season normally flowering in August-September.

The Marsh Mallow has been used for centuries as a food and medicine, and would have originally been introduced to Ireland as such. The plant particularly flourishes in salty wet soils - exactly where I found it in a salty drain! The leaves and roots of the Marsh Mallow are the parts used in herbal medicine, the whole plant is filled with a mild mucilage which when mixed with water is used as a gel to soothe throat and stomach. Marsh Mallow may show up in the health store as tinctures, capsules, ointment/creams and cough/syrups.

The last fling of Summer/Autumn is perhaps provided by a sprawling display of this Japanese Rose (*Rosa rugosa*) on the approach to Loophead in late September!

Winter's wilderness returns ones eyes to the vigorous lively ocean which drenches the senses in its wildly atmospheric microcosm.

In this treeless landscape at Loophead, a browning Winter wilderness sets in, but early signs of a greening Spring to come take hold.

New Years day on Ross Beach - Northern Storm - this intense energy can inspire a refreshing revival!

Rage on New Year's Day!

We thrust ourselves on Ross Beach
against a vicious Northern storm,
driving and roaring onshore,
dragging the powering, frothing waves,
in an atmospheric microcosm,
that catapults the senses
into a state of wild ecstacy.

This wind thrashing, storm bashing
thumps our exposed faces,
like a last line of defence were we,
overpowered as it pounds inland,
leaving the raging waves to finally collide
on the lower stony shore.
thank God it's not a Spring Tide.

Little James and I brave it
to the rockpools,
our eagerness overpowering, our fear,
in our bid to list the inhabiting
creatures, and sub-aqua features,
in our newly named pools.

It's tamer down here,
as the storm rides above us
tearing fiercely through the nearby fields,
we alone with the tidal storm.

The sky high brightness quickly swings
into a low sky blackening fear,
as it fills with rushing heavy clouds,
with a strange pink tinge,
luminosity occupies a low space,
in the fuzzy, wave ridden horizon.

We scamper quickly, time to get out,
highly strung gulls, scream on high,
no angels here, James tears ahead,
head bowed, arched back,
I wish he would hold onto me,
as the gusting storm takes its stronghold,
tossing and pushing us on our exit path.

Deeper thoughts form,
this energy, vitality,
threatening reality,
brightness and darkness,
shadow and light,
A creative storm, reform our wilted Spirit,
deliver us this New Year born.

(2012)

'Storm on the Moor' 2006
Private Collection - Co. Clare

Chapter 6 - The Inspired Artworks

There is a pervasive Spirit, that permeates each work, that I can only associate with the location where I grew up: Loophead. This Spirit presents itself in atmospheric, and elemental depictions that constitute raw vigorous energy, raw wild habitat, continuous movement, and the driving forces that surround the Loophead Landscape. In 'Storm on the Moor' for instance, one is transported to the wild intensity of a vigorous storm bearing down on the open unsheltered moors. Yet in 'Summer Dance on Tufted Moor' there is a frivolous light hearted atmospheric engagement between the crispy breeze from the Ocean and the low flowering vegetation on the Moor top, creating an uplifting dance ritual.

Meanwhile 'Garden of Entangled Freedom' is concerned with the depiction of the dense mesh of growth that prevails in the height of the growing season on the hedgerows and in meadows, with abundance, variety of textures and free entanglements amongst species. A true artist expression of the joy of a wild congregation! 'Seeking Nebulous Treasures' too, is closely associated with abundance, textures and colours, reaching for the clouds, as if they have hidden treasures! This is a playful take on the mostly upwardly growing vegetation. 'Grow to Sun' is concerned with the magnetism of the sun in drawing the flowers from the ground.

'Annual Assembly - Meeting of the Flowers' is a moving depiction of the free reigning flora in the high flowering Season, in an assembly that suggests an annual exchange of floral expression between species encapsulated by their particular dance rituals.

'Un-ravelling Winds of Freedom' and 'Ocean in the Garden' are perhaps more associated with my mothers Summer garden, which grew wonderfully each year until the first salt-laden storms of Autumn blew in from the Ocean, instantly burning the garden. A juxtaposing of both control and freedom in the singular atmospheric element that is the varying strength of the wind is evoked in these works.

'Chemin des Piétons' - (title linked to my new immersion in the French Language!) has a deeply Spiritual feel to it, and it depicts mother and son walking in a flowery environment, inspired entirely by my so-journs with James along the narrow flowery roadsides at Loophead.

'Spring Parade' is to Spring as 'Memories of Summer' is to Summer. 'Spring Parade' aims to present the density of yellow hues that partake in the wonderful early flush of both Dandelion and Daffodil, and the lesser yellow flowers like the Lesser Celandine, and the florets are an artist fusion of all yellow Spring flowers, and personally I find these early flowering fields to be the most uplifting after Winter's dull hues. 'Memories of Summer' - which is part of a series, is carefree, blue-skyed and awash with Summer hues, a depiction that aims to capture that 'feel good' factor of a beautiful sunny day.

Directly referencing Loophead, are the more traditional depictions of the hedgerows, in 'August Hedgerows near Loophead' 'Musical Hedgerows - Summer Breeze' and 'Floral Inclusion Zone near Loophead'

'Summer Garden-November Storm' is a depiction that is inspired by the decimation of my mother's Summer garden in the vicious November storms, whilst the high density work that is the 'Garden of the Spirit of Freedom' simplifies the elements of the flora, the petal-filled breeze, flowing river and dense textures in deeper tonal hues and more subdued movement than normally employed.

'Summer Garden - November Storm' 2006
Private Collection - Co. Dublin

'Vigorous Ocean - Stubborn Rock' 2006
Private Collection - Dublin

'Grow to Sun' 2006
Private Collection - Dublin

'Freedom Blossoms' 2007
Private Collection - Dublin

INSPIRED ARTWORKS

'Summer Dance on Tufted Moor' 2009
Private Collection - Co. Kerry

'Annual Assembly - Meeting of the Flowers' 2009
Public Art - Barefield National School, Co. Clare

INSPIRED ARTWORKS

'Chemin des Piétons' 2009
Private Collection - Co. Clare

'Garden of Entangled Freedom' 2011
Private Collection - Co. Kilkenny

"Seeking Nebulous Treasures" 2011
Private Collection - Cork

'Garden of the Spirit of Freedom' 2010
Private Collection - Dublin

'Unravelling Winds of Freedom' 2010
Private Collection - Waterford

'Ocean in the Garden' 2008
Private Collection - USA

'Spring Parade' 2008
Private Collection - Dublin

INSPIRED ARTWORKS

'Memories of Summer' 2007
Collection of Dromoland Castle

'Florale Inclusion Zone near Loophead' 2006
Private Collection - Co. Kerry

'August Hedgerows near Loophead' 2008
Private Collection - Co. Cork

'Musical Hedgerows - Summer Breeze' 2006
Private Collection - Limerick

Old Man on the Bench

Old man on the bench, you take a rest from life
in the harrowed trench spent,
tilling the earth that surrounds you,
in the fields of toil, fields of joy and scorn,
behind the knitted hedgerows and the scrubby thorn,
nature's defence from storm and ocean's bloated roar.

Old man on the bench, now the gaps in the field
mingle the gaps in your silent memory,
like wading through the rushes of a blind mans field,
ear to the belching and balling of a thundering ocean
as you recall fields of laboured treasures,
harvested and measured,
better than last year or the year of 65.

Old man on the bench, you await new friends
or even a lonesome stranger, eagerly awaiting
a memory exchange, small talk of past and present,

let the world know your relevance,
re-awaken your instinct and experience,
the mercilessness of nature's salty breeze
and icy freeze,
or the ongoing threats of blight and fly,
as you read the threat or promise
of a near and distant sky.

Old man on the bench,
if nobody brings themselves to you today,
your memories silent will remain,
yet infiltrating the airspace
through your breath and eyes,
silently mingling the breeze around you,
the spirit of your vibrant past
communicating with your dear and dead friends,
exchanging energies with stilled lives,
you remain an unquenchable soul,
an indelible life.

(2010)

BIBLIOGRAPHY

Nelson, Charles
Wild Plants of the Burren and the Aran Islands(2008)

Rose, Francis & revised & updated by O' Reilly, Claire
The Wild Flower Key (2006)

Gibbons, Bob
Wildflower Wonders of the World (2011)

Butler, Ken - Crossan, Ken(photographs)
Wild Flowers of the North Highlands of Scotland (2009)

Green, Paul
Flora of County Waterford (2008)

Sayers, Brendan - Sex, Susan
Irelands's Wild Orchids - A Field Guide

Preston, CD, Pearman, DA,& Dines, TD
New Atlas of the British & Irish Flora 2002

bsbi.org.uk
the westernisles.co.uk/wildflowers
gardenorganic.org.uk
carrotmuseum.co.uk
herbalhub.com

wildflowersofireland.net
irishwildflowers.ie
botanical.com
wildflowersofstratclydepark.com
countrysideinfo.co.uk
scotshistoryonline.co.uk
altnature.com
wildseed.co.uk
druidry.org
Alternative-healthzine.com
first-nature.com
celtnet.org.uk
foragingcourses.com
cosmeticsdesign-europe.com
herbsociety.org.uk
agroathlas.ru
plantlife.org.uk
britishwildlife.com
ukwildflowers.com
clarebirdwatching.com
clarebiodiversity.ie
sepmstrata.org
heritagecouncil.ie
complete-herbal.com
herballecacy.com
iwt.ie
irishseedsavers.ie

ACKNOWLEDGEMENTS

There were some critically important people whose combined input, ensured that this publication came to fruition.

Mrs. Mai Magner - my mother, provided the early childhood nature nurturing that awakened my curiosity towards flora, fauna and the seashore. James Madigan, my son, became my constant curious and interesting companion during my field research. Mrs Mary Gibson, my sister, provided regular persuasive encouragement which eventually kick-started this book. Peter Madigan, my husband, was always supportive of our research and my book project and ensured that it would be published.

Paul Green, Botancial Author, BSBI recorder and expedition leader, willingly and enthusiastically brought his expertise to photo confirmation of difficult species. Congella Maguire, Clare Heritage Officer, provided enthusiastic support and important linkages. Stephen Ward of Clare Biodiversity and the Burren beo Trust, provided expert proof reading of the script and offered positive feedback, helpful comments and useful contacts. Dr. Micheline Sheehy Skeffington, Department of Botany and Plant Science, NUI Galway, kindly read the text and made very valuable observations and comments.

The Clare Local Development Company, through its LEADER Programme provided financial support towards the final production costs of this book.

INDEX

Achillea millefolium 58
Achillea ptarmica 58
Allium babingtonii 75
Alternate leaves 24
Althaea officinalis 116
Amphibious Bistort 110
Anagallis Arvensis 106
Anagallis Tenella 35
Angelica sylvestris 99
Anthriscus sylvestris 102
Anthyllis Vulneraria 40
Arctic Tern 13
Arctium minus 59
Armeria maritima 63
Arrow-shaped leaf 25
Atriplex laciniata 56
Atriplex prostrata 71
Aster tripolium 54
Atlantic Ocean 11,27
Babington's Leek 6,21,75,79
Basal Rosette 24
Beta Vulgaris maritima 65
Bell Heather 27,32,57
Bird's-foot Trefoil 37,51,108
Bistort 110
Bittersweet 13,61,67,71
Black Mustard 92
Blackthorn 17
Black Tar Lichen 61
Black Tufted Lichen 61

Bladder Wrack 14
Blymsus rufus 69
Bog Cotton 51,59
Bolboschoenus maritimus 69
Bog Pimpernel 35,51
Bramble 21,47,80,84,116
Brassica rapa 92
Broad-leaf Plantain 61
Broad-leaf Willowherb 104
Buck's horn Plantain 14
Burdock 51,59
Burnet Rose 8,97
Bush Vetch 47
Buttercup 79,98
Cakile maritima 73
Calluna vulgaris 57
Calystegia sepium spp. Roseata 101
Calyx 26
Cardamine pratensis 88
Carrigeen Moss 14,61
Cat's-ear 6,19,32,45
Celandine (Lesser) 87,92,98
Centaurea nigra 110
Centaurium erythraea 31
Cerastium glomeratum 88
Channelled Wrack 14,61
Church of the Little Ark 15,19
Cirsium arvense 112
Cirsium palustre 113
Cirsium vulgare 113

Clasping Stem 25
Cochlearia officinalis 72
Common Centaury 6,13,31,32,33
    Chickweed 88
    Dog Violet 79,86,92
    Mallow 6,76
    Mouse-ear 51,88
    Scurvy grass 13,71,72
    Sorrel 93
    Whitlow grass 88
    Valerian 96
    Vetch 47
Convolvulus soldanella 67
Cordate leaf 24
Corymb 26
Cow Parsley 79,99,102
Cowslip 87
Creeping Thistle 14,79,112
    Tormentil 19,34
Crithmum maritimum 63
Crocosmia x crocosmiiflora 109
Cross-leaved Heath 57
Cuckoo Flower 79,88
Curled Dock 19,61,66,71
Dactylorhiza occidentalis 51
Dandelion 79,85
Daucus carota 33,77
Devil's-bit Scabious 42
Diamond-shaped Leaf 25
Dilisk 14

Dipsacus fullonum 74
Disc Floret 26
Egg Wrack 14
Elder 17,95
Elecampane 6,41
English Stonecrop 6,13,30,31,42
Epilobium hirsutum 104
Erica cinerea 57
Eriophorum angustifolium 59
Euphrasia 43,76
Eyebright 6,43,76
Fleabane 14,51,80,108
Fea's Petrel 13
Fen 19
Festuca rubra 32,36
Filipendula ulmaria 105
Frosted Orache 56,71
Fuchsia 115
Fuchsia magellanica 115
Fulmar 13
Fumitory 79
Furze 79,83
Gannets 13
Geranium robertianum 86
Glaux maritima 68
Gorse 83
Greater Willowherb 6,14,19,80,104
Guillemot 13
Heart-shaped Leaf 24
Heather 32,37,51,57
Hedge Bindweed 19,67,101
Hedge Parsley 99,102
Herb Robert 79,86
Hoary Willowherb 104
Hogweed 79,99,102
Honeysuckle 6,80,89
Hydrocotyle vulgaris 46

Hypochaeris radicata 45
Inula helenium 41
Inter-tidal Zone 14
Irish Marsh Orchid 8,12,19,51
Iris pseudacorus 98
Japanese Rose 117
Jasione montana 30
Kidney Vetch 6,40,51
Kidney-shaped Leaf 23
Kittiwake 13
Knapweed 14,80,110
Lanceolate Leaf 23
Lathyrus pratensis 108
Leaflets 23
Lesser Burdock 59
    Celandine 19,87,92,98
    Centaury 31
    Spearwort 49,51,98
Ligustrum vulgare 101
Linear Leaf 25
Ling 27,29,57
Lobed Leaf 24
Lonicera periclymenum 89
Loophead Lighthouse 12
Lotus corniculatus 37
Lychnis flos-cuculi 91
Lythrum salicaria 103
Malva sylvestris 76
Marsh Mallow 19,116
    Pennywort 46
    Thistle 14,79,114
Meadowsweet 14,19,80,105
Meadow Vetchling 37,47,101,108
Michelmas Daisy 54
Montbretia 8,14,79,80,109
Namurian 11
Navelwort 46

Oblong Leaf 23
Obovate Leaf 23
Odontites vernus 76
Opposite Leaves 24
Orache - Spear-leaved 56,61,71
    - Frosted 56,71
Orange Leafy Lichen 14,61
Oxeye Daisy 80
Paired Leaves 24
Palmate Leaf 23
Pedicel 75
Perennial Sow Thistle 19,61,66,71
Perfoliate Leaf 25
Petal 26
Petiole 25
Pineapple weed 64
Plantago lanceolata 90
Plantago maritima 42
Polygonum amphibia 110
Potentilla anglica 34
Potentilla anserina 49
Potentilla erecta 34
Prickly Sow Thistle 92
Primrose 79,84
Primula veris 87
Primula vulgaris 84
Puffin 13
Pulicaria dysenterica 108
Purple Loosestrife 14,19,80,103
Raceme 26
Ragged Robin 19,79,91
Ragwort 80,114
Ranunculus acris 98

145

Ranunculus ficaria 87
Ranunculus flammula 49
Rape 92
Ray Floret 26
Red Bartsia 71,76
Red Clover 56,79,93
Red Fescue 32,36
Ribbon Weed 14
Ribwort Plantain 79,90
Rock Samphire 13,61,63
Rock Sea Spurrey 13,68,88
Rosa pimpinellifolia 97
Rosa rugosa 117
Rosebay Willowherb 104
Ross Formation 13
Rubus fruticosus 116
Rumex acetosa 93
Rumex crispus 66
Sabine's Gull 13
Sally Bush 79
Sambucus nigra 17,95
Scarlet Pimpernel 6,106
Sea Arrowgrass 51,55
    Aster 8,12,51,54,55,56
    Beet 13,61,65,71
    Bindweed 67
    Campion 8,32,36
    Club Rush 14,69
    Grass 14,61
    Ivory 14,61
    Lettuce 14,61
    Mayweed 13,19,61,64,71

Sea Milkwort 14,61,68
    Pink 12,29,32,42,53
    Plantain 42,90
    Rocket 13,71,73
Sedum anglicum
Self Heal 38
Senecio jacobaea 114
Sepal 26
Shag 13
Shearwater 13
Sheep's-bit 8,13,29,30,51
Silene Uniflora 36
Silverweed 19,37,49,61
Skua 13
Sneezewort 51,58
Solanum dulcamara 67
Sonchus arvensis 66
Sonchus asper 92
Spear-leaved Orache 56,61,71
Spear-shaped Leaf 25
Spear Thistle 14,79,114
Spergularia rupicola 68
Spike 26
Spiral Wrack 14,61
Sticky Mouse Ear 88
St. John's wort 14,80
Succisa pratensis 42
Sugar Kelp 61
Tangle Weed 61
Taraxacum officinale agg. 85
Teasel 71,74
Tendril 23
Thrift 8,12,29,32,42,53
Thymus polytrichus 38
Toothed Leaf 24
Toothless Leaf 24
Torilis japonica 102
Tormentil 32,34,51

Trifoliate Leaf 24
Trifolium pratense 93
Trifolium repens 56
Triglochin maritimum 55
Tripleurospermum maritimum 64
Tufted Vetch 47,48,51,79,101
Ulex europaeus 83
Umbel 26
Umbilicus rupestris 46
Valerian 79,96
Valeriana officinalis 96
Vicia cracca 48
Vicia sativa 47
Viola riviniana 86
Wall Pennywort 46
Whimbrel 13
White Clover 37,51
Whitethorn 17
Wild Angelica 80,99
    Cabbage 92
    Carrot 8,32,33,71,77,99
    Clover 56
    Mallow 71
    Privet 79,101
    Rose 51,97
    Spinach 65
    Thyme 8,12,32,38,42,51
    Turnip 92
Whorl (leaf) 23
Yarrow 51,58
Yellow Flag 79,98

A new horizon unfolds...

Edible Sea Lettuce

James on the rocky shore

Edible Limpets and abundant species & textures

......And so our adventure continues to rock and crevice, ledge and edge of our coastal shore, a treasury of virgin territory to explore..... an ancient formation, grown upon, held onto, lashed upon, waved upon, dreamt on and lived on passively and aggressively, in our midst... perhaps we will tread on our ancestors footsteps, taste its edible offerings and languish in its misty spell, whilst we strive to fulfill our desire to understand its enormous influential being.

Lichens too numerous to mention

There is reflection and deflection of light and shadow

147